SENDEROS 1

Spanish for a Connecte

Writing Proficiency Workbook

ISBN: 978-1-68005-240-4
1 2 3 4 5 6 7 8 9 BB 22 21 20 19 18 17

Table of Contents

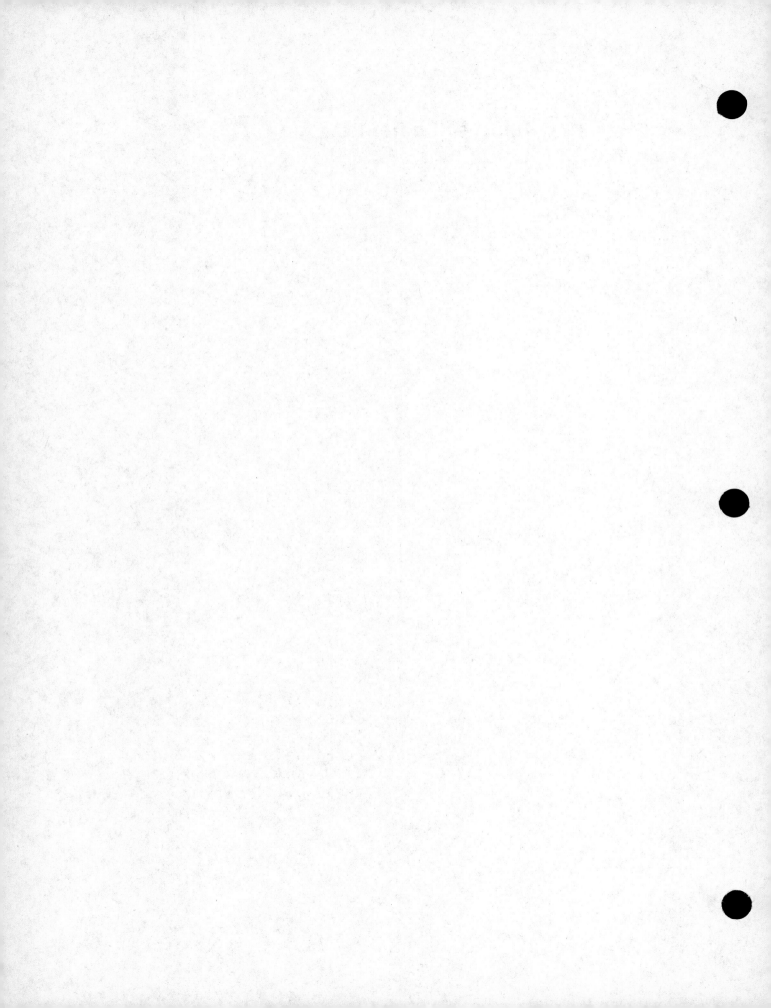

Preface

Enhancing Writing Skills

The goal of the *Writing Proficiency Workbooks* that accompany **Senderos** is to put the skill of writing at the forefront and to hone writing skills and confidence, building in a progressive manner from word- and sentence-level production in **Senderos 1** up to full-length essays and presentation writing in **Senderos 5**.

Sequencing and Pacing

Each workbook has been carefully sequenced pedagogically in order to provide guidance in the many facets of writing, including how to make appropriate word choices, write well-crafted sentences, organize cohesive paragraphs, and sequence information chunks logically. Grammatical structures studied in the **Estructura** sections of each lesson are supported with additional practice, review, and recycling beyond the scope of the apparatus found in both the textbook and the *Cuaderno de práctica.*

Writing-specific strategies are introduced and practiced in the *Writing Proficiency Workbooks*. These strategies, which are additional to those presented in the main text, are designed to strengthen skills already acquired in traditional English or language arts courses. As a whole, they focus on information germane to writing in any academic field, although some focus specifically on differences between the grammar, syntax, and stylistics of Spanish and English. These strategies include creating simple sentences, scaffolding to create complex and compound sentences, brainstorming, freewriting, paraphrasing, summarizing, and many more.

The five levels of *Writing Proficiency Workbooks* coordinate with the American Council on the Teaching of Foreign Language's writing proficiency guidelines. Each level includes writing tasks specified by ACTFL as corresponding to the following proficiency levels:

Senderos 1	Novice Low to Novice High
Senderos 2	Intermediate Low, Intermediate Mid
Senderos 3	Intermediate Mid, Intermediate High
Senderos 4	Intermediate High, Advanced Low
Senderos 5	Advanced Low, Advanced Mid

Note that these proficiency designations refer to the writing tasks outlined by ACTFL and not necessarily to the complete mastery of the task at that level. Students' abilities to complete these tasks will vary, and the grading rubrics found in the level answer keys provide more information about how to evaluate the mastery of a given writing task.

In accordance with the ACTFL guidelines for World-Readiness Standards for Learning Languages, most of the activities found in the *Writing Proficiency Workbooks* cue students in English to avoid providing key vocabulary or structures that might inform student production.

Focusing on the Writing Genres

Assignments created for the *Writing Proficiency Workbooks* represent writing in a variety of genres found in many real-world scenarios, gradually moving from personal writing (with which beginning students are more comfortable) to more academic and professional tasks. The goal is to promote confidence in writing production by first focusing on low-stakes subjects that are familiar and interesting. The activities then move toward more purposeful academic writing: summarizing readings, critiquing and expressing opinions, persuading, and producing presentational texts based on research. By the end of **Senderos 5**, writing tasks include producing an essay of several pages, thus moving beyond mastery of the once-revered five-paragraph essay template to more open-ended, thought-driven writing.

Tying Reading to Writing

Some of the exercises in the *Writing Proficiency Workbooks* involve summarizing readings found in the **Senderos** textbook. Summarizing is a writing skill that is useful across the curriculum, both in this course and in future language courses. In relation to the **Cultura** readings, for instance, writing tasks may involve first producing a summary of a sentence or two and progressively building toward writing a paragraph-length summary of the reading. Summarizing activities may be adapted to individual courses, expanding upon the apparatus provided here so as to pertain to other level-appropriate readings that students may locate in novels, newspapers, or online.

Integrating Individual and Collaborative Writing

Though the focus of the *Writing Proficiency Workbooks* is individual writing, there are many opportunities for pair and group collaboration as well. Many students find sharing their writing to be an embarrassing, intimidating, or unthinkable task; however, collaborative writing has become a much-sought-after skill in the job market, and students need to develop a "comfort zone" with such collaborative tasks. To this end, we have included activities that lend themselves to peer-reviewing and peer-editing practice, as well as one overtly collaborative writing exercise per lesson in all levels except Level 1, where the writing tasks are too basic for consistent collaboration. The early collaborative activities help foster sharing with peers. When instructors feel the time is right for higher-stakes sharing, any of the writing apparatus can be assigned for peer-reviewing or peer-editing.

Lección 1

1 ***Why Does Writing by Hand Matter?*** The world is mostly paperless. If something isn't digital in format and viewable on a device, it virtually goes unnoticed. Why, then, is the **Senderos** *Writing Proficiency Workbook* available only in printed (paper) format? There are two very good reasons.

First, the act of writing by hand *improves your recall of what you are writing* because it forces you to focus on the physical task of writing. Writing by hand is slower than writing by digital means, which gives you more time to think about what you are writing. Typing on a keyboard, even if you're a terrible typist, does not require the same level of concentration as manipulating a pen or pencil across a sheet of paper. Many studies have concluded this: From kindergarteners who are learning the alphabet by print-writing it to college students who take notes by hand rather than by device, the act of writing improves the learning process and helps you retain information longer.

Second, writing by hand helps you *avoid the pitfalls of constant distractions* . . . or, more accurately, the *temptation* to be distracted. If you compose on a tablet, laptop, or phone, you can easily and quickly shift your attention away from what you are writing to any number of unrelated tasks: checking status updates, watching a cute cat video, texting your friends that you'll be missing band practice, or sneaking in one more try at Level 6 of a new game.

So when it comes time to do the assignments in this workbook, put aside the devices and make it all about you, a pencil, and the printed page. Take small chunks of time, like 20 minutes, for doing the assignments. Some of the activities are broken into steps called **Etapas**, so you don't have to complete the whole activity all at once. You'll be amazed at how much you can accomplish in a short time if you devote 100 percent of your energy and attention to the writing assignment.

THINK ABOUT IT! You have an assignment to write 15 sentences. You figure this should take you about 20 to 30 minutes, no more. So you get started. You write one sentence . . . it's so awesome that you decide to treat yourself to a snack. Ten minutes later, you get back to writing another couple of sentences. You're on a roll. Then your phone blows up: there's a Twitter war between two friends, and everybody else is getting into it, too. You read the tweets, respond to a few, and send a text to one of the friends involved. Suddenly, the half hour you needed to finish the assignment has been wasted and you've written only three and a half sentences. Plus, you're so amped up from the online fight that your concentration is shot.

What can you do differently next time?

Nombre ______________________ Fecha ______________________

2 **Sopa de letras** Find 20 vocabulary words from **Lección 1** in the grid, looking horizontally, vertically, or diagonally. Circle them in the puzzle and put a check mark next to the clue in the list below. **¡Buena suerte!** (*Good luck!*)

C	O	N	P	E	R	M	I	S	O	B	D	U	M
M	A	C	G	L	Í	R	J	A	N	V	I	K	E
N	E	N	C	A	N	T	A	D	O	Z	C	E	N
U	D	F	A	N	T	E	G	P	C	Y	C	L	O
E	L	Q	U	D	O	C	E	C	H	É	I	V	S
V	S	D	Ó	L	Á	P	I	Z	E	B	O	T	D
O	S	C	I	N	T	U	R	E	S	L	N	U	I
T	C	H	U	A	M	É	X	I	C	O	A	R	E
Q	H	Ú	L	E	B	U	E	N	I	C	R	I	Z
U	A	M	T	R	L	H	O	U	S	E	I	S	K
I	U	O	A	F	R	A	X	C	A	D	O	T	I
É	L	D	A	T	Q	S	Á	L	T	O	D	A	L
N	U	V	E	I	N	T	I	C	I	N	C	O	S
E	O	Y	R	M	B	A	U	T	O	B	Ú	S	E
R	G	A	P	D	E	L	A	M	A	Ñ	A	N	A

1. al norte (*north*) de los Estados Unidos
2. Perdón. = ________. (2 palabras)
3. *something a boy says after being introduced*
4. A las 9:00 P.M.: Buenas ________.
5. *half a dozen*
6. Hay estudiantes en la ________.
7. Adiós. = ________.
8. *something to write with*
9. *a.m.* = ________ (3 palabras)
10. *two dozen plus one*
11. ¿Qué hay de ________?
12. *used to look up words*
13. país al sur (*south*) de los EE.UU.
14. ________ pronto
15. *an even dozen*
16. ¿De ________ es el cuaderno?
17. 3:50 = las cuatro ________ (2 palabras)
18. *a person on vacation*
19. *you might ride one to school*
20. por ________

3 **Letras revueltas: La O es Omnipresente.** The following words come from the **vOcabulariO** in **LecciÓn 1**. The letters are scrambled, but the **O's** are in their place. Unscramble the remaining letters and fill in the spaces to spell out each word or phrase. The slash indicates the start of a new word: for example, **¿QUÉ / HORA / ES?**

1. **A A H N P R S T T**	___ ___ ___ ___ ___ / ___ ___ O ___ ___ O.
2. **E M N S S V**	___ O ___ / ___ ___ ___ O ___.
3. **B A D E Í N S U S**	___ ___ ___ ___ O ___ / ___ ___ ___ ___.
4. **C C D N U T R**	___ O ___ ___ ___ ___ ___ O ___
5. **A D L S S U**	___ ___ ___ ___ ___ O ___
6. **F T A F G Í R A**	___ O ___ O ___ ___ ___ ___ ___ ___
7. **A E F P R R S**	___ ___ O ___ ___ ___ O ___ ___
8. **C C D E H I I**	___ ___ ___ ___ ___ O ___ ___ O
9. **C E I P R R T U**	___ ___ ___ ___ ___ O / ___ ___ ___ O
10. **A D D E I Í M**	___ ___ ___ ___ O ___ ___ ___
11. **C E I M N P R S**	___ O ___ / ___ ___ ___ ___ ___ ___ O
12. **D C C A I I I N R**	___ ___ ___ ___ ___ O ___ ___ ___ ___ O
13. **C D E**	___ O ___ ___
14. **A A C L N R S S T U**	___ O ___ / ___ ___ ___ / ___ ___ ___ ___ ___ O.
15. **A F P R R V**	___ O ___ / ___ ___ ___ O ___

Lección 1

4 **Letras revueltas: ¡La E* Es ExcElEntE!** The following words come from the **Vocabulario** in LEcción 1. The letters are scrambled, but the E's are in their place. Unscramble the remaining letters and fill in the spaces to spell out each word or phrase. The slash indicates the start of a new word: for example, ¿QUÉ / HORA / ES?

1. A A B D N R S S T U ___ ___ E ___ ___ ___ / ___ ___ ___ ___ E ___.
2. I I I N S S T V ___ E ___ ___ ___ ___ ___ É ___ ___
3. A D H N O Q U Y ___ ___ / ___ ___ ___ / ___ E / ___ ___ É.
4. A C L S U E ___ ___ ___ E ___ ___
5. A D I N S T T U E ___ ___ ___ ___ ___ ___ ___ ___ E
6. A A C D N N T O E ___ ___ ___ ___ ___ ___ ___ ___.
7. I G A L M N T U ___ ___ ___ ___ ___ ___ E ___ ___ E.
8. A D H N O Q U U V Y ¿___ ___ É / ___ ___ ___ / ___ E / ___ ___ E ___ ___?
9. C C I L N Ó ___ E ___ ___ ___ ___ ___
10. B D I I N N O S V ¡___ ___ E ___ ___ E ___ ___ ___ ___ ___!
11. A N O P R S T T ___ E / ___ ___ E ___ E ___ ___ ___ / ___...
12. G Í L M O O S S T U E ___ / ___ ___ ___ ___ ___ / E ___ / ___ ___ ___.
13. D D D N Ó R S ¿___ E / ___ ___ ___ ___ E / E ___ E ___?
14. B M N O R ___ ___ ___ ___ ___ E
15. D I M N O S Z ___ E ___ ___ ___ / ___ ___ E ___

* The letter *e* is the most used letter in the Spanish language, occurring in almost 14 percent of all words. *E* is followed closely by *a*, which occurs in around 13 percent of Spanish words. Can you guess what the least common letters are? *W* and *k*, which only appear in words borrowed from other languages (like **Wáshington** from English and **kilómetro** from Greek).

Nombre ______________________ Fecha ______________________

5 **¿Cuánto ya sabes?** **ETAPA 1:** Match each capital city in Column A with the correct country in Column B. Write the letter in the blank space. The first one is done for you. **Pista** (*Clue*): If you aren't sure of a country's capital, consult the maps on pages viii–xiii in the **Senderos 1** textbook.

A	B
1. Quito *e*	a. Argentina
2. Washington DC _____	b. Canadá
3. San José _____	c. Costa Rica
4. Buenos Aires _____	d. Cuba
5. Santo Domingo _____	e. Ecuador
6. Ciudad de México _____	f. España
7. Ottawa _____	g. Estados Unidos
8. San Juan _____	h. México
9. Madrid _____	i. Puerto Rico
10. La Habana _____	j. República Dominicana

ETAPA 2: Now write a complete sentence stating what the capital of each country is.

modelo

España

La capital de España es Madrid. or
Madrid es la capital de España.

1. Puerto Rico ______________________
2. la República Dominicana ______________________
3. Cuba ______________________
4. Ecuador ______________________
5. Argentina ______________________

6

Categorías ETAPA 1: Write each of the following words under the appropriate heading according to the category where it belongs: **Gente** (*People*), **Lugares** (*Places*), **Cosas** (*Things*), or **Otras palabras y expresiones** (*Other words and expressions*).

abrazo	en punto	igualmente	páginas	por favor
bienvenidos	escritora	lápices	país	regular
capital	escuelas	maleta	pasajeros	señoritas
conductor	hombre	mano	plaza	universidad

Gente	Lugares
1. ______	1. ______
2. ______	2. ______
3. ______	3. ______
4. ______	4. ______
5. ______	5. ______

Cosas	Otras palabras y expresiones
1. ______	1. ______
2. ______	2. ______
3. ______	3. ______
4. ______	4. ______
5. ______	5. ______

ETAPA 2: Once you have completed the lists, go back and add the appropriate definite article (**el, la, los, las**) to each of the words you wrote in the **Gente, Lugares,** and **Cosas** categories.

Nombre ______________________ Fecha ______________________

Lección 1

7 **Estrategia: *Working with Cognates—Nouns*** In the **Lectura** section of your textbook, you read about *cognates*, which are words in two different languages that look very similar and have similar meanings. Some of the vocabulary words you learned in **Lección 1** are cognates: **el mapa, el/la turista,** and **la computadora**, for example.

As you continue learning Spanish, you will encounter many cognates in texts you read. Cognates are important for two reasons: they help you understand a text better and they help you increase your vocabulary. Chances are, after studying this chapter, you'll remember the words **mapa, turista,** and **computadora!** And as your vocabulary grows, your ability to write your thoughts in Spanish will improve.

> **THINK ABOUT IT!** As you read your own writing aloud, remember that even when a Spanish word looks very much like its English "cousin," it is still pronounced using the rules of Spanish pronunciation.

PRÁCTICA: Look for patterns as you answer the following questions about Spanish–English cognates.

1. **la nacionalidad** = *nationality*; **la comunidad** = *community*. Based on this information, what do you think the following words mean?

   a. la universidad ______________________

   b. la personalidad ______________________

   c. la electricidad ______________________

   Now, complete the following general rule: Spanish words that end in **-dad** are usually [*what gender?*] ____________. The English words that correspond to them end in [*what letters?*] ____________.

2. **la conversación** = *conversation*; **la nación** = *nation*. Based on this information, what do you think the following words mean?

   a. la administración ______________________

   b. la evaluación ______________________

   c. la composición ______________________

   d. la pronunciación ______________________

   Now, complete the following general rule: Spanish words that end in **-ción** are usually [*what gender?*] ____________. The English words that correspond to them end in [*what letters?*] ____________.

3. Some Spanish–English cognates are easy to recognize because they are spelled exactly the same or differ only by one or two letters; for example, the words **video**, **perdón**, and **profesora**. Based on this information, what do you think the following words mean?

   a. el teléfono ______________________

   b. el automóvil ______________________

   c. el sándwich ______________________

   d. la novela ______________________

   e. el apartamento ______________________

   f. la música ______________________

   g. el programa de televisión ______________________

   h. el chocolate ______________________

   i. el dólar ______________________

   j. la cámara digital ______________________

Nombre ______________________ Fecha ______________________

8 **Preguntas y respuestas.** For each group, match the questions from Column A with the appropriate answers from Column B. Then write out each mini-dialogue on the lines provided. The first dialogue in **Grupo 1** is done for you.

Grupo 1	
A	**B**
¿A qué hora es la presentación de Mateo?	No, nosotras somos turistas.
¿Cómo se llama el chico de Arizona?	No es un cuaderno. Es el diario de Mariana.
¿Son ustedes estudiantes?	No, es doctor.
¿El señor Saldívar es profesor de historia?	No sé.
¿De quién es el cuaderno?	Es a las dos y quince.

1. *¿A qué hora es la presentación de Mateo?*
   Es a las dos y quince.
2. ______________________
3. ______________________
4. ______________________
5. ______________________

Grupo 2	
A	**B**
¿Hay un mapa de los Estados Unidos?	No, es del profesor Rivas.
¿De dónde es la profesora?	No, es Madrid.
¿La maleta es de la estudiante?	Se llama Felipe Pérez.
Barcelona es la capital de España, ¿verdad?	Ella es de Caracas, Venezuela.
¿Quién es el chico?	Sí, hay uno de Norteamérica en la Lección 1.

6. ______________________
7. ______________________
8. ______________________
9. ______________________
10. ______________________

Grupo 3	
A	B
¿Pablo es famoso?	Es el Instituto de Tecnología.
¿Qué hay de nuevo?	Tres chicas son de México y él es de Ecuador.
¿Cómo se llama la escuela?	Nada. ¿Y tú?
¿Hay diecinueve computadoras en la clase?	Sí, es un actor profesional.
¿Cuántos estudiantes de Latinoamérica hay?	No, hay veintitrés.

11. ______________________________

12. ______________________________

13. ______________________________

14. ______________________________

15. ______________________________

9 **¿Qué dicen ellos?** What would you and the following people say in each situation?

1. **a.** You overhear an older gentleman speaking Spanish. You say hello, tell him your name, and ask him where he is from.

   ____

   b. How might the gentleman respond?

   ____

2. **a.** Your Spanish teacher introduces you to Mrs. Rodríguez. What does your teacher say?

   ____

   b. How do you respond?

   ____

   c. How might Mrs. Rodríguez respond to what you say?

   ____

3. **a.** You want to know how many books there are on the table (**en la mesa**).

   ____

   b. Your classmate says there are thirteen books and one dictionary.

   ____

   c. You ask who the dictionary belongs to.

   ____

   d. Your classmate says it's the teacher's.

   ____

4. **a.** You greet a friend and ask him how he is.

   ____

   b. How might your friend reply?

   ____

5. **a.** A friend of yours says bye and that she'll see you later.

   ____

   b. How might you respond?

   ____

6. **a.** You say "Hey" to get your younger sibling's attention and then ask what time it is.

   ____

   b. How might he/she reply if it's late in the evening?

   ____

   c. How might he/she reply if it's the afternoon?

   ____

10 **Correcciones** Each of the following brief dialogues contains errors in spelling, punctuation, missing or misplaced accents, or missing words. If a line of dialogue contains errors, rewrite it and correct the errors. If the line is correct, rewrite it as is and place a checkmark before it.

¡Atención! New words that are translated in parentheses do NOT contain errors.

1. — Holla, professor Olmos.
   — ____________________
   — Buenos dias, Enrique. ¿Como estás?
   — ____________________
   — Bien, gracias, ¿y ustéd?
   — ____________________
   — Muy bien. Hasta pronto.
   — ____________________
2. — De dónde es Ud., senora Uribe?
   — ____________________
   — Soy de Costa Rica, de la capital.
   — ____________________
   — Mi (*My*) profesora español es de Costa Rica.
   — ____________________
3. — Melissa, te presento a Rita Sánchez.
   — ____________________
   — Mucho gusto, señor Sánchez.
   — ____________________
   — Gusto es mio, Melissa.
   — ____________________
4. — Cuantos estudiantes hay en la clase?
   — ____________________
   — Hay veinticuatro.
   — ____________________
   — Y como se llama el profesor?
   — ____________________
   — Se llama Sr. Rivas.
   — ____________________
5. — ¿De quién es el cuaderno?
   — ____________________
   — Es Raúl.
   — ____________________
   — Y los lapizes?
   — ____________________
   — Son de Raúl también (*also*).
   — ____________________

Lección 2

1 **Sendero de palabras** Follow the path from beginning to end. Use the clues (pistas) below to fill in the missing words from this chapter. Words read either horizontally, left to right or vertically, top to bottom.

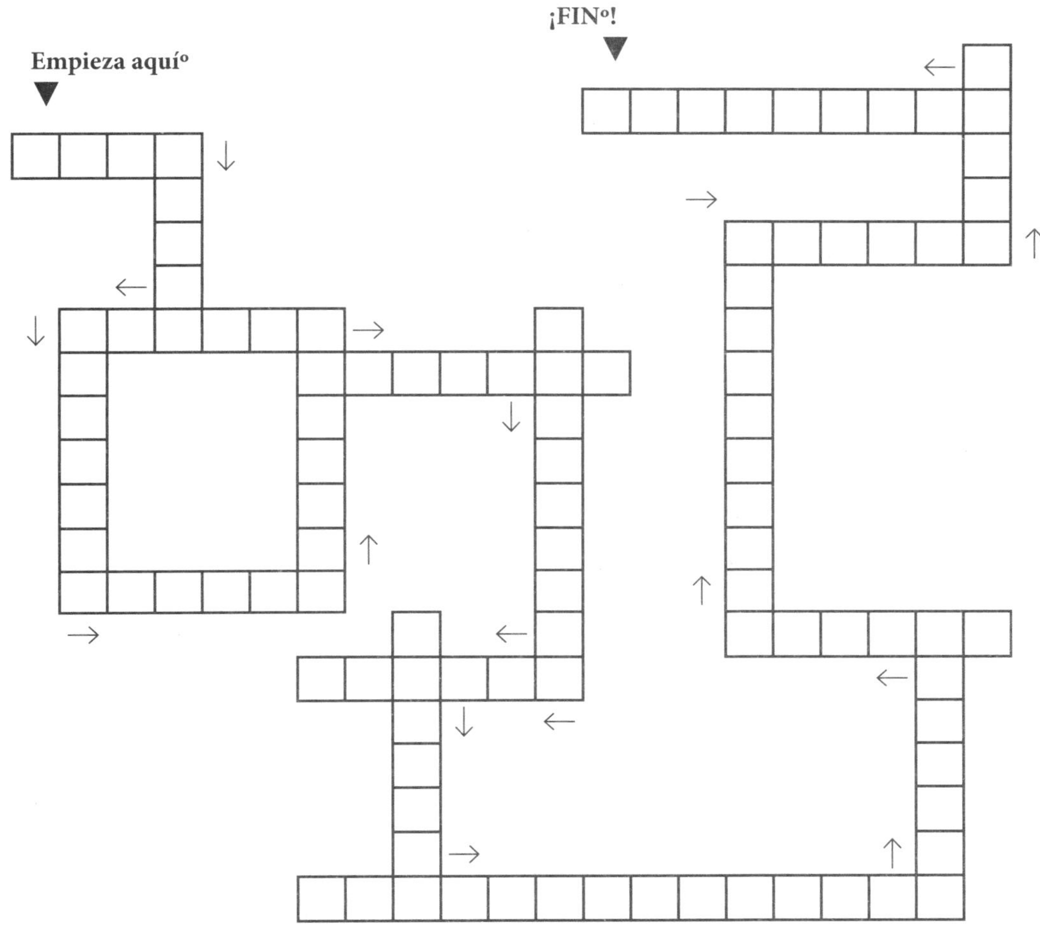

°Empieza aquí *Start here* °FIN *END*

PISTAS

a. Se usa (*It is used*) con una pizarra.

b. *now*

c. La pasajera desea ________ a Europa.

d. un día de la semana

e. una mesa y cuatro ________

f. Hay dos ________ que indican (*indicate*) la hora.

g. un idioma o lengua

h. lo opuesto (*opposite*) de **preguntar**

i. El tren necesita ________ a tiempo (*on time*).

j. No es una puerta, es una ________.

k. *to the left of* (cuatro palabras)

l. lo opuesto de **detrás de:** ________ de

m. *Where to?*

n. 1.090 en palabras

o. el día después del lunes

p. ¿Cuántas clases ________ tú?

q. el ________ de clase

Lección 2

2 **Una nube de palabras** A *word cloud* (**nube de palabras**) is a visual representation of the most commonly used words in a text. The size of each word indicates how frequently it was used: the larger the word, the more times it appeared in the text. The word cloud below shows some of the most commonly used English words in a language textbook.

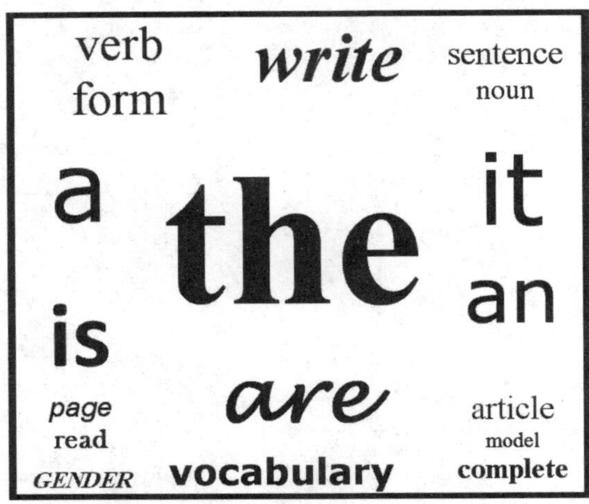

ETAPA 1: Scan the first two lessons of your **Senderos 1** textbook. What do you *think* the 20 most used Spanish words are? List them below. (You do not have to count the words . . . just estimate!)

1. ________	8. ________	15. ________
2. ________	9. ________	16. ________
3. ________	10. ________	17. ________
4. ________	11. ________	18. ________
5. ________	12. ________	19. ________
6. ________	13. ________	20. ________
7. ________	14. ________	

ETAPA 2: Now draw a word cloud using your list from **Etapa 1.** Remember to make the most commonly used words larger than the less common words.

Nombre ______________________ Fecha ______________________

3

Estrategia: *Writing Spanish Sentences* Spanish sentences follow many of the same rules that English sentences do.

Rule 1: A complete sentence includes a *subject* and a *verb*. The subject tells who or what the sentence is about, and the verb indicates the action or a state of being. In the examples that follow, the subjects are in boldface and the verbs are underlined.

Gaby canta.	**Ernesto y yo** conversamos mucho.
Gaby sings.	*Ernesto and I chat a lot.*

¡Atención! When a sentence or series of sentences contains several verbs, you do not have to state the subject with each verb unless the subject changes or is not clear from the context of the sentence. For example:

Gaby canta. Pero no baila.

Ernesto y yo conversamos mucho y estudiamos juntos (*together*).

BUT

Todos (*Everybody*) llegan a casa a las seis. Cenas a las seis y media, pero cena a las nueve.

In the first two examples, the verbs **baila** and **estudiamos** do not need explicit subjects because we understand from context that those verbs refer to **Gaby** and **Ernesto y yo**, respectively. However, in the third example, the verb **cenas** clearly refers to the subject **tú**—you can tell that by the **-as** ending. But the verb **cena** has no clear subject (it could be either **usted**, **él**, or **ella**). One must be provided for the sentence to be understood:

Cenas a las seis y media, pero **Carlota** (**ella**) **cena** a las nueve.

PRÁCTICA 1: Is the subject of each verb in boldface clear? If so, write it in the space. If it is not, write *unclear*.

1. Elena **trabaja** poco (*a little*) y **descansa** mucho.
   trabaja: ______________________ **descansa:** ______________________
2. **Desayunamos** a las siete y **cenan** a las seis.
   Desayunamos: ______________________ **cenan:** ______________________
3. **Es** profesora.
   Es: ______________________
4. **Tomas** dos clases de ciencia.
   Tomas: ______________________
5. El profesor Gómez **enseña** la clase de matemáticas.
   enseña: ______________________
6. **Compro** un cuaderno y unos lápices en la librería.
   Compro: ______________________
7. **Escucha** música ahora, pero Pilar **desea** hablar con él.
   Escucha: ______________________ **desea:** ______________________
8. Lalo y Tim **regresan** a las siete.
   regresan: ______________________
9. Pero no **hablan** inglés, ¿verdad?
   hablan: ______________________
10. La clase de contabilidad **termina** pronto (*soon*).
    termina: ______________________

Nombre ______________________ Fecha ______________________

Rule 2: A complete sentence expresses a complete thought. The sentence **Gaby canta.** (*Gaby sings.*) is a complete thought. However, sentences like **Gaby busca.** (*Gaby looks for.*) and **La universidad está.** (*The university is.*) do not make sense because they lack enough information to express a complete thought.

INCOMPLETE	COMPLETE
✗ Gaby busca.	✓ Gaby busca **un libro.**
✗ La universidad está.	✓ La universidad está **en la capital.**

Lección 2

You must always make sure the sentences you write in Spanish (1) clearly indicate who or what the subject of each verb is and (2) express complete thoughts.

PRÁCTICA 2: Indicate whether each sentence is complete or incomplete. If it is incomplete, rewrite it with more information to make it complete.

1. El escritorio al lado de la ventana. COMPLETE INCOMPLETE
   está
2. Mirta y tú desean. COMPLETE INCOMPLETE
   enseñar
3. La señora Sáenz necesita. COMPLETE INCOMPLETE
   agua
4. Benito trabaja en Madrid ahora. COMPLETE INCOMPLETE
5. Buenos Aires está, ¿verdad? COMPLETE INCOMPLETE
   en Argentina
6. Andrés y Rosario en la biblioteca. COMPLETE INCOMPLETE
   estudian
7. No estudio los sábados. COMPLETE INCOMPLETE
8. Ahora Laura y Antonia buscan. COMPLETE INCOMPLETE
   a la Señora García
9. Tomás y yo a las ocho. COMPLETE INCOMPLETE
   estudiamos
10. Te presento a mi (*my*) compañera de clase. COMPLETE INCOMPLETE

Nombre _______________ Fecha _______________

PRÁCTICA 3: Write a follow-up sentence for each sentence given. If the subject stays the same, omit it in the second sentence. If it changes, clearly state the new subject. Make sure your sentences express a complete thought. Follow the model.

modelo

Descansamos por la tarde.

YOU WRITE, FOR EXAMPLE: Trabajamos por la noche. *or*
Andrea descansa por la mañana.

1. El chico se llama Julio.
   estudia a las ocho de la mañana
2. Elena termina la tarea.
   ____
3. Pablo y yo llevamos los libros a la oficina (*office*) de la profesora.
   ____
4. Papá explica las teorías de Einstein.
   ____
5. Caminas al estadio.
   ____
6. Yolanda toma matemáticas y música.
   ____
7. ¡Yo no soy artista!
   ____
8. Los estudiantes no escuchan en clase.
   ____
9. Necesito tomar una clase de arte los sábados.
   ____
10. Uds. bailan muy bien.
    ____

4 **Asociaciones** ETAPA 1: Write the verb from **Lección 2** that you associate with the following words and phrases.

1. el arte, lápices, papel ______________________
2. un diálogo, hablar con amigos ______________________
3. un restaurante, la noche ______________________
4. antes de (*before*) una prueba ______________________
5. estar exhausto/a, una silla cómoda (*comfortable*) ______________________
6. una pregunta, el teléfono ______________________
7. tomar café, los cereales, la mañana ______________________
8. la música, el ballet ______________________
9. de las 9 a las 5, ganar dinero (*earn money*) ______________________
10. hacer cola (*stand in line*), el autobús ______________________

ETAPA 2: Now select at least five of the verbs from **Etapa 1** and write a sentence for each one. Challenge yourself to use more than one verb in some sentences! Consult the checklist on page 87 to help you write complete sentences and to look for possible errors in them.

1. ______________________
2. ______________________
3. ______________________
4. ______________________
5. ______________________
6. ______________________
7. ______________________
8. ______________________
9. ______________________
10. ______________________

Nombre ______________________ Fecha ______________________

5 **¿Sustantivo o verbo?** You don't have to be a grammar expert in order to write well, but you should have some understanding about how words work in a sentence.

- A *noun* (**sustantivo**) names a person, place, thing, or idea.
- A *verb* (**verbo**) indicates an action or a state of being.

ETAPA 1: Sort the following words into categories: **Sustantivos**, **Verbos**, or **Otras palabras** (*Other words*). Write each one in the appropriate column.

ahora	**cerca de**	**esperar**	**llegas**	**porque**	**tarea**
bailo	**chau**	**está**	**matemáticas**	**profesor**	**trimestre**
boletos	**compran**	**gracias**	**mucho**	**semana**	
busca	**con**	**gusta**	**nombre**	**sobre**	
caminamos	**cuarto**	**hoy**	**página**	**son**	

Sustantivos	
1. ________	6. ________
2. ________	7. ________
3. ________	8. ________
4. ________	9. ________
5. ________	

Verbos	
1. ________	6. ________
2. ________	7. ________
3. ________	8. ________
4. ________	9. ________
5. ________	

Otras palabras	
1. ________	6. ________
2. ________	7. ________
3. ________	8. ________
4. ________	9. ________
5. ________	

ETAPA 2: Once you have completed the **Sustantivos** list, go back and add the appropriate definite article to each noun.

Nombre ______________________ Fecha ______________________

ETAPA 3: Now write five sentences using a noun and a verb from the lists in **Etapa 1.** Use each word only once. Consult the checklist on page 87 to help you write complete sentences and to look for possible errors in them.

1. ______________________
2. ______________________
3. ______________________
4. ______________________
5. ______________________

Lección 2

6 **Familias de palabras** A *word family* refers to a group of words that are derived from the same root and are related in meaning. In English, for example, *bake, baker*, and *bakery* are all associated with making delicious treats, and *dentist*, *dental*, and *dentistry* are all related to teeth. Members of a word family can be nouns, verbs, or adjectives.

You have already learned several pairs of Spanish words that belong to the same family. Think about how these pairs of words are related:

- **el libro** *and* **la librería**
- **la computadora** *and* **la computación**
- **la hora** *and* **el horario**
- **el/la estudiante** *and* **estudiar**
- **el papel** *and* **la papelera**

Recognizing related words will help you guess at or figure out their meanings and remember them later.

Palabras relacionadas: The first word in each group is a word you have learned. What do you think the new words in boldface mean? Write their English meaning in the space.

1. el borrador — **borrar** [*verb*] ______________________
2. la economía — **económico** [*adjective*] ______________________
3. descansar — **un descanso** [*noun*] ______________________
4. practicar — **la práctica** [*noun*] ______________________
5. la geografía — **geográfico** [*adjective*] ______________________
6. trabajar — **el trabajo** [*noun*] ______________________
7. cenar — **la cena** [*noun*] ______________________
8. el arte — **el/la artista** [*person*] ______________________
   artístico [*adjective*] ______________________
9. dibujar — **un dibujo** [*noun*] ______________________
10. viajar — **el/la viajero/a** [*person*] ______________________
11. estudiar — **estudioso** [*adjective*] ______________________
12. desayunar — **el desayuno** [*noun*] ______________________

Nombre ______ Fecha ______

7 **El aula de clase** **ETAPA 1:** What's in the classroom shown in the illustration? What is each thing next to, above, behind, etc.? Write 7 sentences that describe the scene. Use the verbs **hay** and **estar**, prepositions that indicate location, and numbers.

1. ______
2. ______
3. ______
4. ______
5. ______
6. ______
7. ______

ETAPA 2: Now describe one of the classrooms in your school. It can be your Spanish class or another class. What's in the room? What is the room near? Name the class in sentence 1, and then write seven more sentences about that classroom. Consult the checklist on page 87 to help you write complete sentences and to look for possible errors in them.

1. Es el aula de clase de ______
2. ______
3. ______
4. ______
5. ______
6. ______
7. ______
8. ______

Lección 2

Nombre ______________________ Fecha ______________________

8 **¿Lógico o ilógico?** Read each sentence carefully. If the sentence is logical, circle LÓGICO. If it is not, circle ILÓGICO and rewrite the sentence, making any changes needed so that your new sentence is logical. Follow the model.

modelo

Adela contesta el estadio. **LÓGICO** **(ILÓGICO)**

YOU WRITE, FOR EXAMPLE: *Adela contesta la pregunta.*

1. Jorge estudia matemáticas porque le gustan los números. LÓGICO ILÓGICO

____

2. Mañana viajamos a la contabilidad. LÓGICO ILÓGICO

____

3. El borrador regresa a las dos. LÓGICO ILÓGICO

____

4. El laboratorio está cerca de las ciencias. LÓGICO ILÓGICO

____

5. El compañero de Antonio es estudiante. LÓGICO ILÓGICO

____

6. Desayunas con Bárbara a la medianoche. LÓGICO ILÓGICO

____

7. Los profesores necesitan comprar una física. LÓGICO ILÓGICO

____

8. Tomamos la clase de periodismo en el laboratorio. LÓGICO ILÓGICO

____

9. Javier y Ana preparan el reloj. LÓGICO ILÓGICO

____

10. Esperan el autobús delante de la escuela. LÓGICO ILÓGICO

____

9 **¿Quién lo hace?** For each sentence, replace the underlined subject with a new subject. Make all necessary changes. Follow the model.

¡Atención! When you change the subject, also change the verb form so it agrees with the new subject.

modelo

Nosotros tomamos la clase de química.

YOU WRITE, FOR EXAMPLE: *Alina toma la clase de química.*

1. Linda desea comprar ocho libros.
2. Los estudiantes practican el diálogo.
3. Tú viajas a España mañana.
4. Héctor y Roberto miran el programa.
5. Yo estoy en la cafetería.
6. ¿Qué compra el señor García en la librería?
7. Nosotros preparamos tacos y burritos.
8. Los profesores conversan en el laboratorio.
9. ¿Cuándo llegas tú a casa?
10. La chica lleva una mochila azul (*blue*).
11. Mi (*My*) compañero de clase trabaja en un restaurante.
12. Yo necesito dos lápices.
13. Mónica y Alexis no explican bien la lección.
14. A las siete de la mañana los chicos esperan el autobús.
15. Eduardo y yo caminamos a la biblioteca.

Nombre ______________________ Fecha ______________________

10 **¿Qué hacen?** ETAPA 1: In each numbered space 2–5, write the name of a person. It can be someone you know, a famous person, or an imaginary person. Sentences in number 1 will be about you.

ETAPA 2: For each person indicated, write three sentences to tell what he or she does, does not do, or likes. Use a variety of verbs—you've learned almost 40 different ones so far! Include as much information in each statement as you can. Then, consult the checklist on page 87 to help you write complete sentences and to look for possible errors in them.

Lección 2

modelo

nombre: *Pedro*

a. *Pedro no desayuna en la cafetería.*

b. *Él viaja mucho a San Juan.*

c. *Hoy a las cuatro estudia en la biblioteca.*

1. Yo
   a. ______________________
   b. ______________________
   c. ______________________
2. nombre: ______________________
   a. ______________________
   b. ______________________
   c. ______________________
3. nombre: ______________________
   a. ______________________
   b. ______________________
   c. ______________________
4. nombre: ______________________
   a. ______________________
   b. ______________________
   c. ______________________
5. nombre: ______________________
   a. ______________________
   b. ______________________
   c. ______________________

Nombre ____________________ Fecha ____________________

11 **Reescribir** Rewrite each sentence below, substituting new information for the underlined words. Then, when you can, write two new versions of each sentence. Follow the model.

modelo

Eduardo cena <u>en la cafetería</u>.
YOU WRITE, FOR EXAMPLE: *Eduardo cena en casa.*
or Eduardo cena a las siete.
or Eduardo cena con Linda y Mariana.

1. Tomás dibuja <u>un mapa de España</u>.
2. Los estudiantes escuchan <u>a la profesora</u>.
3. ¡Pilar canta <u>en la biblioteca!</u>
4. Me gusta estudiar <u>con Alberto</u>.
5. El escritorio está <u>al lado de la ventana</u>.
6. El señor Montes es profesor <u>de arte</u> en San Juan.
7. Elena trabaja <u>en la cafetería</u>.
8. Regresas <u>a medianoche</u>, ¿verdad?

Lección 2

Nombre Fecha

9. Buscamos el diccionario… no está en la mochila.

10. Necesito explicar el problema.

11. Antonia no contesta el teléfono.

12. Los turistas de Argentina llegan a las cuatro.

13. ¿Cuándo compras el libro de biología?

14. La librería está allá, cerca del estadio.

15. A las tres menos cuarto termina la clase de física. (*Make substitutions for two items here.*)

16. ¿Te gusta enseñar historia?

17. Manolo viaja a California el jueves. (*Make substitutions for two items here.*)

Lección 2

Nombre ______________________ Fecha ______________________

12 **La primera semana de clases** ETAPA 1: The following numbered sentences form a short narrative. First, familiarize yourself with the glossed words. Then read each sentence carefully. Once you understand each sentence individually, go back and read the entire selection.

1. El regreso° a la escuela es un evento muy emocionante° y también muy estresante°.
2. El año° académico consiste en nueve meses° de trabajo para los estudiantes y para los profesores.
3. Por eso°, la primera semana de clases es muy importante.
4. Todos° tienen que acostumbrarse° a un nuevo horario y a una nueva rutina diaria°.
5. Los días son muy ocupados° y a veces° no hay tiempo libre°.
6. Los alumnos necesitan dedicarse° a sus libros.
7. Hay mucha tarea y muchos exámenes.
8. Para los profesores, hay trabajos° para corregir° y los preparativos para las lecciones.
9. Pues, ¡todos a trabajar°! Hasta las vacaciones de verano°...

El regreso *The return* emocionante *exciting* estresante *stressful* año *year* meses *months* Por eso *For that reason* Todos *Everybody* acostumbrarse *to get used to* rutina diaria *daily routine* ocupados *busy* a veces *at times* tiempo libre *free time* dedicarse *dedicate themselves* trabajos *papers* corregir *to correct* ¡todos a trabajar! *everyone get to work!* verano *summer*

ETAPA 2: Answer each question about the narrative in **Etapa 1.** You might want to review the activities *Working with Cognates* in **Lección 1** (p. 7), and **Familias de palabras** (p. 20), and *Writing Spanish Sentences* (pp. 15–16) in this lesson before you begin.

1. What is the subject of each of the following sentences?

   a. *sentence 1:* ______________________

   b. *sentence 2:* ______________________

   c. *sentence 5:* ______________________

   d. *sentence 6:* ______________________

2. Write the English meaning of the following cognates.

   a. **académico** (*sentence* 2) ______________________

   b. **consiste** (*sentence* 2) ______________________

   c. **importante** (*sentence* 3) ______________________

   d. **vacaciones** (*sentence* 9) ______________________

3. Think about the meaning of *sentence 6*. What other vocabulary word could you substitute for **Los alumnos** that would NOT change the meaning of the sentence?

   ____

Lección 2

4. What verbs from *Lección 2* belong to the same word family as the following words?

   a. **el regreso** (*sentence 1*) _______________

   b. **trabajo** (*sentence 2*) _______________

   c. **los preparativos** (*sentence 8*) _______________

5. Write the four words found in the sentences that are related to the calendar.

   a. _______________

   b. _______________

   c. _______________

   d. _______________

Nombre ______________________ Fecha ______________________

Lección 3

1 **La oración escondida** Use the clues below to fill in each line of the puzzle. When you are finished, the letters in the shaded boxes will reveal a sentence that completes the dialogue below. Write the hidden sentence in the space provided.

1.
2.
3.
4.
5.
6.
7.
8.
9.
10.
11.
12.
13.
14.
15.

Pistas:

1. Ramón _____ treinta años.
2. El estudiante no _____ la lección.
3. Un hombre de Quito es _____.
4. El autobús parte (*leaves*) en dos minutos... debes tener mucha _____.
5. lo opuesto de **gordo**
6. una chica muy joven
7. Tengo que escribir un _____ para la clase de inglés.
8. Es correcto, tienes _____.
9. El sushi y el wasabi son comidas (*foods*) _____.
10. color asociado con los dólares
11. color asociado con la tiza
12. de Berlín, por ejemplo
13. Hoy Elsa no _____ a sus clases. Está en casa.
14. lo opuesto de **fácil**
15. Necesito dormir (*sleep*) porque tengo mucho _____.

Diálogo:

— La cantante Shakira es bella, delgada, talentosa, rica (*rich*)... ¡lo tiene todo (*she has everything*)!

— No es verdad... ¡____!

2 **Asociaciones** ETAPA 1: Write the verb or adjective from **Lección 3** that you associate with the following words and phrases.

1. Adele, los príncipes (*princes*) William y Harry ______
2. la ventana, la puerta, el libro ______
3. permitir que tu hermano use tus cosas ______
4. papel, lápiz, la mano, un ensayo ______
5. color oscuro (*dark*), la noche ______
6. el café, una Coca-Cola, la sed ______
7. tener hambre, un sándwich, cenar ______
8. el libro **Senderos**, una novela, los textos ______
9. la pizza, el Coliseo, Roma, Versace ______
10. los abuelos, tener muchos años ______

ETAPA 2: Now select at least six of the vocabulary words from **Etapa 1** and write a sentence for each one. Be creative. Consult the checklist on page 87 to help you write complete sentences and to look for possible errors in them.

1. ______
2. ______
3. ______
4. ______
5. ______
6. ______

Nombre ______________________ Fecha ______________________

3 **¿Sustantivo, verbo o adjetivo?** **ETAPA 1:** Sort the following words into categories: **Sustantivos**, **Verbos**, or **Adjetivos**. Write each one in the appropriate column.

abren	china	guapos	mismo	recibe
apellidos	compartir	hambre	nietas	rubio
aprende	cuñado	hay	pequeño	sitio
asisto	decidimos	joven	periodista	vengo
azul	fea	leen	prisa	verde
bueno	gente	médica	próximo	vives

Sustantivos	Verbos	Adjetivos
1. ________	1. ________	1. ________
2. ________	2. ________	2. ________
3. ________	3. ________	3. ________
4. ________	4. ________	4. ________
5. ________	5. ________	5. ________
6. ________	6. ________	6. ________
7. ________	7. ________	7. ________
8. ________	8. ________	8. ________
9. ________	9. ________	9. ________
10. ________	10. ________	10. ________

ETAPA 2: Now write seven sentences. Each sentence must contain at least two words from the lists above. Consult the checklist on page 87 to help you write complete sentences and to look for possible errors in them.

1. ______________________________
2. ______________________________
3. ______________________________
4. ______________________________
5. ______________________________
6. ______________________________
7. ______________________________

Lección 3

4 **Familias de palabras.** The first word in each group is a word you have learned. What do you think the new words in boldface refer to? Write their English meaning in the space.

1. alto/a — **la altura** [*noun*] ______
2. el/la periodista — **el periodismo** [*noun*] ______
3. comprender — **la comprensión** [*noun*] ______
4. inteligente — **la inteligencia** [*noun*] ______
5. interesante — **interesar** [*verb*] ______
6. describir — **la descripción** [*noun*] ______
7. difícil — **la dificultad** [*noun*] ______
8. importante — **la importancia** [*noun*] ______
   importar [*verb*] ______
9. beber — **la bebida** [*noun*] ______
10. el/la bisabuelo/a
    el/la nieto — **el/la bisnieto/a** [*person*] ______

Nacionalidades y países

11. alemán, alemana — **Alemania** [*país*] ______
12. francés, francesa — **Francia** [*país*] ______
13. inglés, inglesa — **Inglaterra** [*país*] ______
    Gran Bretaña [*país*] ______
14. italiano/a — **Italia** [*país*] ______
15. japonés, japonesa — **Japón** [*país*] ______
16. ruso/a — **Rusia** [*país*] ______

5

¿Lógico o ilógico? Read each sentence and decide if it makes sense or not. If it does, write **Es lógico.** If it does not, rewrite the sentence so it does make sense.

modelo

Mi abuelo tiene veinticinco años.
YOU WRITE, FOR EXAMPLE: Mi abuelo tiene ochenta años.

1. Cuando tengo sed, como algo (*something*).
____
2. ¡Alana tiene un novio guapo y feo!
____
3. El joven azul es canadiense.
____
4. La profesora debe preparar el examen final.
____
5. Mi hermano abre la puerta porque quiere (*wants*) ser médico.
____
6. Sus hijos pequeños enseñan física en la universidad.
____
7. Me gusta escuchar la música gorda.
____
8. Tenemos que asistir a la nuera a las tres.
____
9. El cuñado amarillo de Ana habla español muy bien.
____
10. Abel y Pablo toman las mismas clases.
____
11. Ustedes viven en una gente cerca de la biblioteca, ¿verdad?
____

Nombre ______________________ Fecha ______________________

12. Un escritorio importante es el autor del libro.

____

13. Los tíos de David vienen el sábado para visitar a su familia.

____

14. Su apellido conversa con el programador porque hay un problema con su computadora.

____

15. Natalia busca un restaurante delgado.

____

16. El estadio corre después de las clases.

____

Lección 3

6 **¿Quién lo hace?** For each sentence, replace the underlined subject with a new subject. Make all necessary changes. Follow the model.

¡Atención! When you change the subject also change the verb form so it agrees with the new subject.

modelo

Adela tiene miedo de los zombis.

YOU WRITE, FOR EXAMPLE: *Nosotros tenemos miedo de los zombis.*

1. La cafetería abre a las siete de la mañana.

____

2. Mis abuelos viven en un apartamento pequeño.

____

3. Sus primos vienen hoy.

____

4. Tú aprendes a bailar salsa, ¿no?

____

5. Yo no asisto a las clases todos los días.

____

6. ¿Qué tiene Adolfo en su mochila?

____

7. Nosotros debemos comprar pan y leche (*bread and milk*).

____

8. Los muchachos reciben y escriben muchos textos.

____

9. ¿Qué bebes tú cuando tienes sed?

____

10. La periodista lee muchos artículos.

____

11. Doña Hilda cree en los espíritus (*spirits*).

____

12. Yo soy muy simpático/a, pero no comparto mis cosas.

____

13. Raúl y Hernán no comprenden el francés.

____

14. Andrea y yo decidimos cenar en el café.

____

15. Los niños malos corren en la escuela.

____

16. Mi nieto inteligente aprende los números y el alfabeto.

____

7 **Estrategia: *Using Idea Maps*** Read the **Escritura** section of your **Senderos 1** textbook (p. 108) before completing this activity.

ETAPA 1: Add more ideas to each mind map.

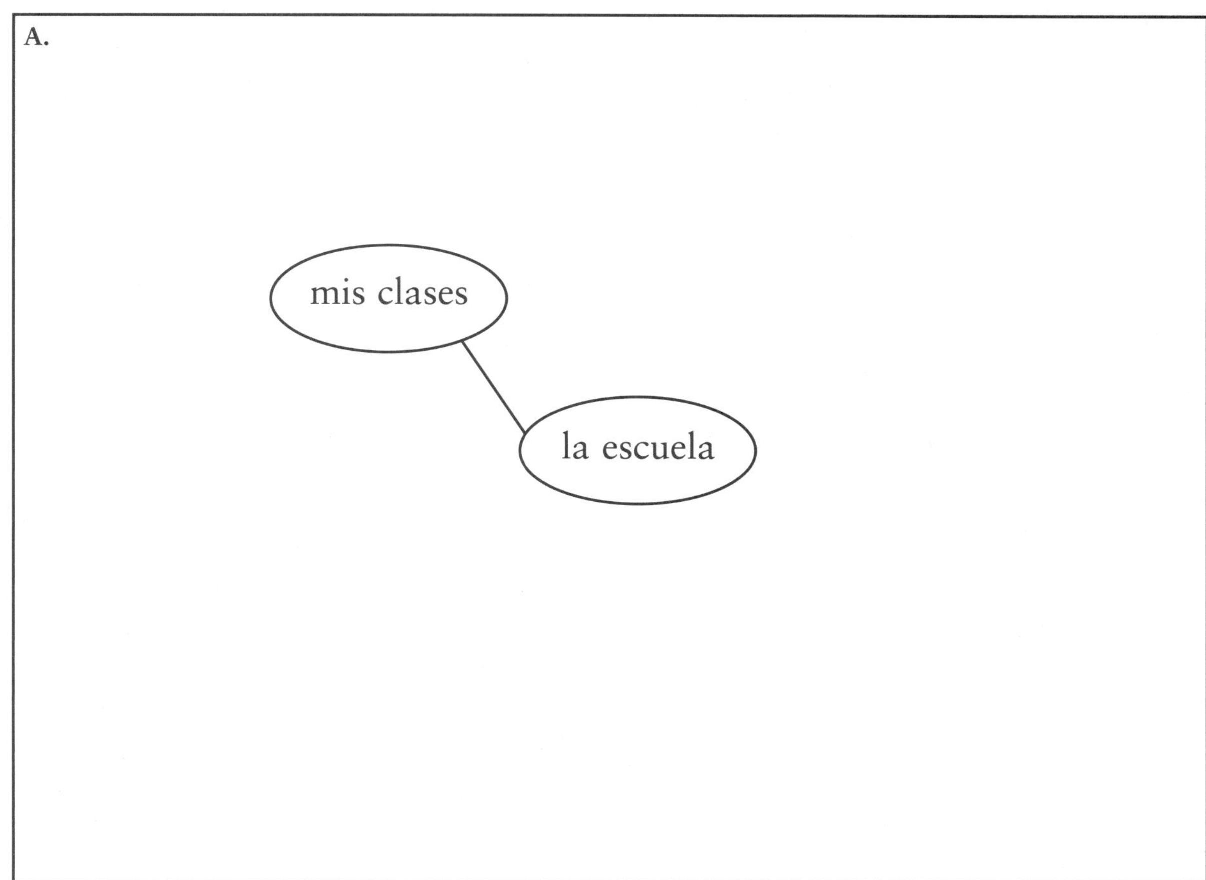

Nombre ______________________ Fecha ______________________

ETAPA 2: Now, using the ideas you generated in your idea maps in **Etapa 1,** write at least six complete sentences about each topic. Consult the checklist on page 87 to help you write complete sentences and to look for possible errors in them.

A. La escuela

1. ______________________
2. ______________________
3. ______________________
4. ______________________
5. ______________________
6. ______________________

B. En casa

1. ______________________
2. ______________________
3. ______________________
4. ______________________
5. ______________________
6. ______________________

Nombre ______________________ Fecha ______________________

8 **Tu familia imaginaria** ETAPA 1: Create a small diagram, mind map, family tree, or list that tells who the members of your "fantasy family" are. They can be real members of your family or famous people you admire: actors, authors, athletes, whoever. Your fantasy family must consist of at least five members other than you. Jot notes next to each member of your family; you will use them in the next **Etapa.**

ETAPA 2: Write three sentences to tell what each member of your fantasy family is like, what he or she does and doesn't do, what he or she likes or doesn't like, and so on. Use **-er** and **-ir** verbs as well as the **-ar** verbs you learned in **Lección 2**. Include as much information in each statement as you can. The following words may be useful.

atlético/a *athletic*	**religioso/a** *religious*
cómico/a *funny*	**rico/a** *rich*
famoso/a *famous*	**talentoso/a** *talented*

modelo

nombre: Patricia Heaton, madre
Mi madre imaginaria es Patricia Heaton. Es bonita y muy cómica...

1. nombre: ______________________
   a. ______________________
   b. ______________________
   c. ______________________
2. nombre: ______________________
   a. ______________________
   b. ______________________
   c. ______________________

Lección 3

3. nombre: ____________
   a. ____________
   b. ____________
   c. ____________
4. nombre: ____________
   a. ____________
   b. ____________
   c. ____________
5. nombre: ____________
   a. ____________
   b. ____________
   c. ____________

Lección 3

9

Más y más... ETAPA 1: Write an ending for each sentence by saying that another person has more or does more than the person stated. Use vocabulary related to family and numbers in your responses. Follow the model.

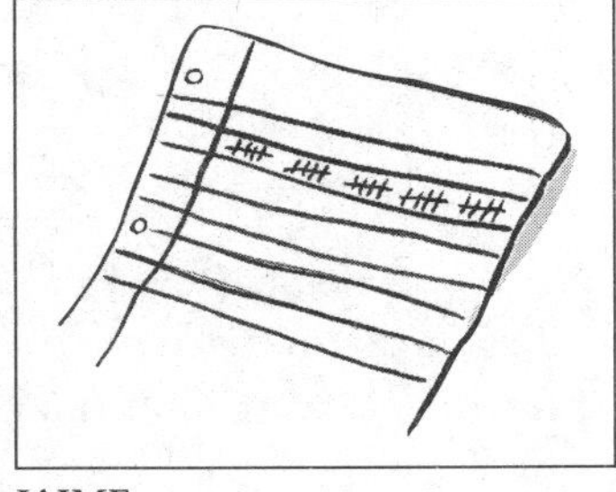

JAIME

modelo

Después del juego (*game*), tengo quince puntos, pero...
YOU WRITE, FOR EXAMPLE: Después del juego, tengo quince puntos, pero mi primo Jaime tiene veinticinco puntos.

1. Beatriz aprende cien palabras nuevas (*new*) de vocabulario, pero...
____
2. Lees dos novelas por (*per*) semana, pero...
____
3. La Sra. Márquez corre dos kilómetros, pero...
____
4. Recibimos cincuenta mensajes de texto en una hora, pero...
____

5. Tengo tres amigos chinos, pero...

6. Claudia y Cindy comprenden dos idiomas, pero...

7. La periodista escribe doscientas palabras por minuto en su computadora, pero...

8. Mi hermano bebe un vaso de leche (*glass of milk*), pero...

9. Tienes dieciséis años, pero...

10. Elisa compra una mochila roja, pero...

11. Asistimos a siete clases por día, pero...

12. El programador trabaja sesenta horas por semana, pero...

ETAPA 2: Now write three more sentences that are totally original. Follow the pattern of the sentences in **Etapa 1**.

1.

2.

3.

10 **Estrategia: *Recognizing the Word Order of Spanish Sentences*** As you have already learned, a complete Spanish sentence requires three things:

1. a subject
2. a verb
3. additional information for the sentence to make sense (the rest of the sentence)

One difference between Spanish sentences and English sentences is that the word order in Spanish is much more flexible than the word order in English. Look first at the following English sentences and think about whether each one sounds right or wrong.

A. Simona opens the door.

B. Opens Simona the door.

C. Opens the door Simona.

You probably came to the conclusion that only sentence **A** sounds right and that **B** and **C** are wrong. This is because the vast majority of English sentences follow the pattern ***subject + verb + the rest of the sentence***, as in *Simona opens the door*. Any other word order seems strange.

This is not the case in Spanish, where the order of the sentence parts can vary. For example, the following variations are all correct.

D. Simona abre *la puerta*. **subject** + verb + *the rest of the sentence*

E. *La puerta* abre **Simona.** *the rest of the sentence* + verb + **subject**

F. Simona *la puerta* abre. **subject** + *the rest of the sentence* + verb

Although the word order of sentence **D** is the most common, **E** and **F** are also correct in Spanish.

As you read and learn more Spanish, you will find sentences that vary in word order. The activities that follow will help you practice and get used this variety.

PRÁCTICA 1: The following sentences are written in the most common word order. Rewrite each one twice using a different word order each time. Use the variations of **Simona abre la puerta** above (sentences D–F) as a model.

1. Elías comparte su cuarto.
   a. _______________
   b. _______________
2. Su hermana mira un video.
   a. _______________
   b. _______________
3. Trini y Pedro leen el periódico (*newspaper*).
   a. _______________
   b. _______________
4. Los señores Takahara son japoneses.
   a. _______________
   b. _______________

5. Nosotros escribimos un ensayo.

   a. ______

   b. ______

6. Jorge trabaja en un restaurante alemán.

   a. ______

   b. ______

7. Elsa visita a su tía Hortensia.

   a. ______

   b. ______

PRÁCTICA 2: Rewrite each sentence so that it follows the common ***subject + verb + the rest of the sentence*** pattern.

1. Vive con sus primos Eduardo.

   ______

2. Come el niño con las manos.

   ______

3. A las nueve termina la clase.

   ______

4. Tiene que estudiar Manolo para el examen.

   ______

5. Come Lidia en la cafetería.

   ______

6. Llega tarde (*late*) el autobús de Cuenca.

   ______

Nombre ______________________ Fecha ______________________

11 **Reescribir** Rewrite each sentence below twice, substituting new information for the underlined words. In one of your sentences, vary the ***subject + verb + the rest of the sentence*** pattern. Follow the model.

modelo

Carlos escribe la tarea.

YOU WRITE, FOR EXAMPLE: *Carlos escribe en la pizarra.*
or *Carlos escribe muy bien.*
or *Escribe Carlos con una pluma roja.*
or *Escribe en su diario Carlos.*

1. Los muchachos aprenden español.
2. Adelina decide tomar el autobús.
3. Roberto compra un suéter (*sweater*) feo.
4. Su novia es una ingeniera importante.
5. Mis parientes viven en Panamá.
6. ¡Mira (*Look*)! Ana tiene la misma mochila.
7. A las siete el Sr. Vásquez corre en el parque.
8. Debes abrir la maleta, ¿verdad?
9. Compartimos un sándwich grande.

Lección 3

10. Necesito leer la novela de Juan León Mera.

11. ¡Ay, el niño escribe una mala palabra!

12. ¿Cuándo vienes de la capital?

13. Uy (*Ugh*), la pasajera es muy antipática.

14. Sarita tiene miedo de los perros (*dogs*).

15. ¿Cómo describes a tu familia?

16. Todavía no comprenden el problema.

Nombre ______________________ Fecha ______________________

12 **Hoy te presento a...** **ETAPA 1:** You will write a character sketch about a person you know. First decide whom you will write about. Then, fill in the following information about that person. Write complete sentences.

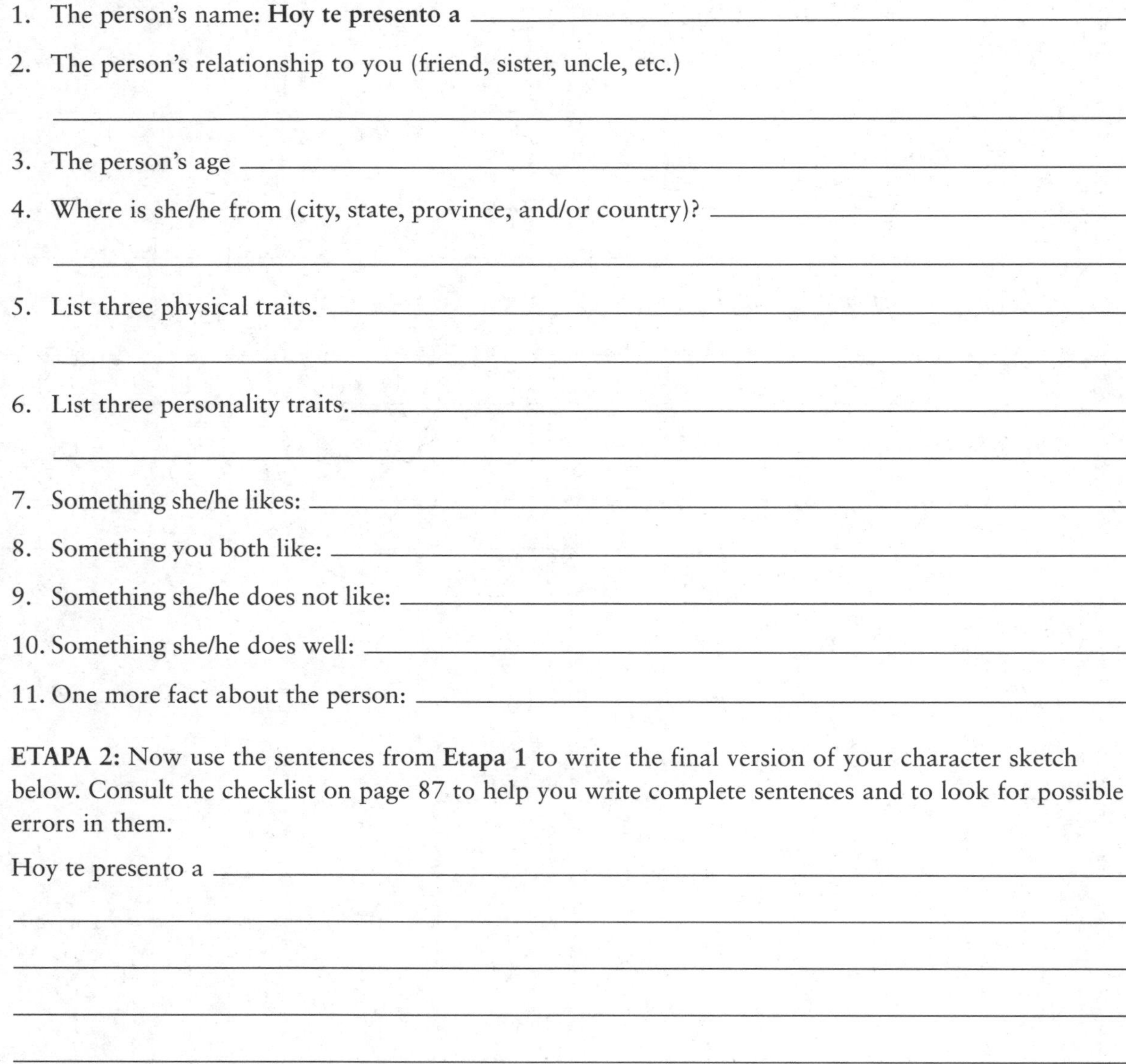

1. The person's name: **Hoy te presento a** ______________________
2. The person's relationship to you (friend, sister, uncle, etc.) ______________________
3. The person's age ______________________
4. Where is she/he from (city, state, province, and/or country)? ______________________
5. List three physical traits. ______________________
6. List three personality traits. ______________________
7. Something she/he likes: ______________________
8. Something you both like: ______________________
9. Something she/he does not like: ______________________
10. Something she/he does well: ______________________
11. One more fact about the person: ______________________

ETAPA 2: Now use the sentences from **Etapa 1** to write the final version of your character sketch below. Consult the checklist on page 87 to help you write complete sentences and to look for possible errors in them.

Hoy te presento a ______________________

Lección 4

1 **Crucigrama.** Solve the following crossword puzzle with words and expressions from this chapter.

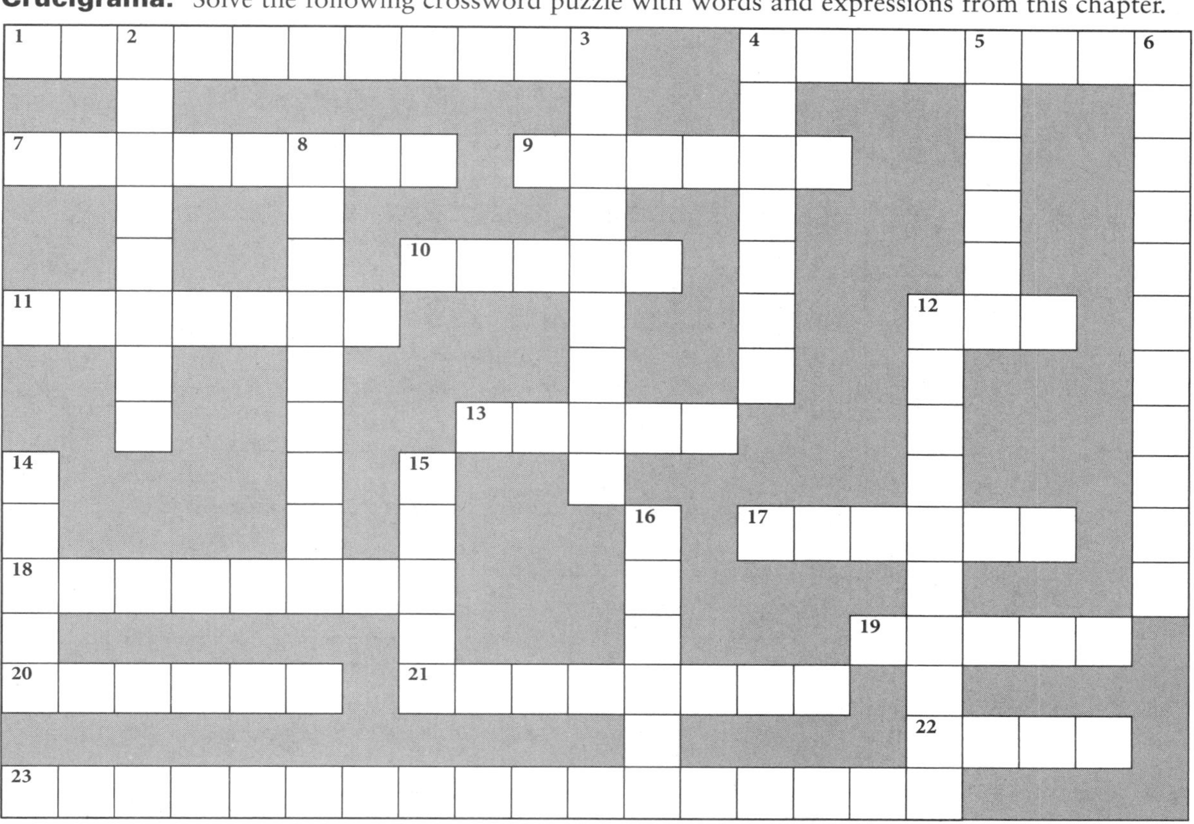

HORIZONTAL

1. sábado y domingo (3 palabras)
4. en el cine ahora y más tarde (*later*) en DVD
7. andar en ________
9. Mucha gente trabaja en el ________.
10. declarar, expresar
11. deporte de los Yankees, los Cubs, los Royals…
12. ir: ellos ________
13. Alicia patina en ________.
17. Se usa (*It is used*) para jugar baloncesto, tenis, vóleibol, etc.
18. No es la verdad. Son ________.
19. Enrique ________ en el océano.
20. Los niños no ________ instrucciones cuando juegan un juego nuevo (*new*).
21. el esquí ________
22. deporte con 18 hoyos (*holes*)
23. En Yahoo! y en Gmail puedes leer tu ________. (2 palabras)

VERTICAL

2. deporte que practicas en la piscina
3. el fútbol ________
4. evento deportivo
5. Pedro no abre el libro. ________ el libro.
6. A ellos les gustan los deportes.
8. el resultado (*result*) de **buscar**
12. *World of Warcraft*, por ejemplo
14. *Let's go!* = ¡________!
15. Hilda ________ en la plaza después de cenar.
16. Decir 1, 2, 3, etc.

Nombre ____________ Fecha ____________

Lección 4

2 **La oración escondida** Use the clues below to fill in each line of the puzzle. When you are finished, the letters in the shaded boxes will reveal a sentence that completes the dialogue. Write the hidden sentence in the space provided.

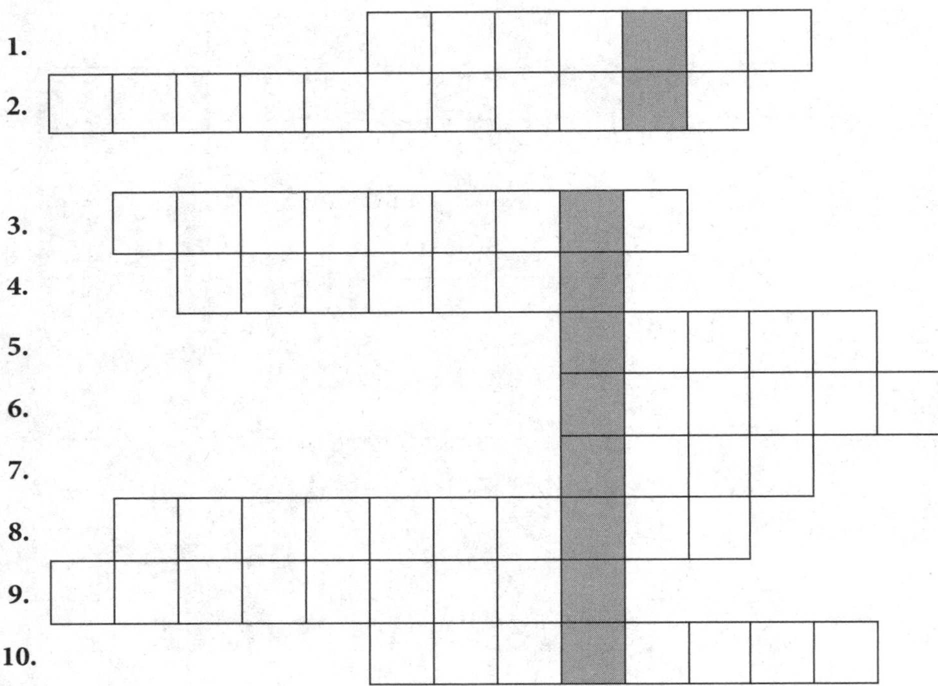

1. lo que haces en línea o en hielo (*ice*)
2. *New York Times, El Nuevo Herald*
3. Frida Kahlo, Picasso, Dalí
4. deporte (*sport*) del Real Madrid y del Barça
5. el Prado de Madrid
6. Olive Garden o Chipotle
7. deporte de Rafael Nadal y de Serena Williams
8. forman un equipo
9. ciudad mexicana en la Bahía de Campeche
10. deporte de Michael Phelps

Diálogo:

— ¿Por qué siempre come mucho postre (*dessert*) el tío Enrique?

— ¡Porque ______________________________!

3 **Asociaciones** ETAPA 1: Write the word or phrase from **Lección 4** that you associate with the following words and phrases.

1. *Buscando a Dory, Guardianes de la Galaxia*, el premio (*award*) Óscar ______________________
2. sábado, domingo, descansar ______________________
3. Colorado, las montañas, Lindsey Vonn ______________________
4. la bicicleta, un deporte olímpico, el Tour de Francia ______________________
5. empezar, lo opuesto de terminar ______________________
6. descansar, al lado de la piscina, broncearse (*to tan*) ______________________
7. los turistas, el arte moderno, los dinosaurios ______________________
8. participar en los deportes, jugar ______________________
9. muchos lugares en Washington DC, la Estatua de la Libertad, la Isla Ellis ______________________
10. deporte popular canadiense, la Copa Stanley ______________________

ETAPA 2: Now select at least six of the vocabulary words from **Etapa 1** and write a sentence for each one. Be creative. Consult the checklist on page 87 to help you write complete sentences and to look for possible errors in them.

1. ______________________
2. ______________________
3. ______________________
4. ______________________
5. ______________________
6. ______________________

4 **Estrategia: *Using a Bilingual Dictionary*** The very best way for you to learn Spanish is to master the words presented in your textbook first. But let's be realistic: there are going to be times when you need to look up a new word or two in order to express what you want to say. But, **¡Atención!** When you do this, you should:

- follow the guidelines in the **Escritura** section of your textbook (p. 144) whenever you look up a new word,
- limit the number of new words you look up to avoid problems, and
- *never* rely on a translation site or software for an accurate result. (Keep in mind the example of the word *racket* in the **Escritura** text.)

PRÁCTICA: Use a bilingual dictionary to look up the following words related to **los pasatiempos**. For nouns, include the appropriate definite article. Then write a sentence using each word.

1. golf clubs ______

   ______
2. (*game*) score ______

   ______
3. puck (*for playing hockey*) ______

   ______
4. cathedral ______

   ______
5. coach (*person*) ______

   ______
6. to participate in ______

   ______
7. ticket (*for an event, a performance, etc.*) ______

   ______

Nombre ______________________ Fecha ______________________

Lección 4

5 **Familias de palabras.** The first word(s) in each group is an expression you have learned. What do you think the new words in boldface refer to? Write their English meaning in the space.

1. jugar
   el/la jugador(a) — **el juego** [*noun*] ______________________
2. esquiar, el esquí — **el/la esquiador(a)** [*person*] ______________________
3. el deporte
   deportivo/a — **el/la deportista** [*person*] ______________________
4. comenzar — **el comienzo** [*noun*] ______________________
5. la diversión — **divertido/a** [*adjective*] ______________________
6. preferir — **la preferencia** [*noun*] ______________________
7. recordar — **el recuerdo** [*noun*] ______________________
8. repetir — **la repetición** [*noun*] ______________________
9. almorzar — **el almuerzo** [*noun*] ______________________
10. nadar
    la natación — **el/la nadador(a)** [*person*] ______________________
11. suponer — **una suposición** [*noun*] ______________________
12. contar (*to tell*) — **un cuento** [*noun*] ______________________
13. leer, la lectura — **el/la lector(a)** [*person*] ______________________
14. la mentira — **mentiroso/a** [*adjective*] ______________________
    mentir [*verb*] ______________________

6 **Estrategia: *Avoiding Unclear Sentences*** In Lección 2 you learned about the basic parts of a Spanish sentence:

1. a subject
2. a verb
3. additional information for the sentence to express a complete thought (the rest of the sentence)

A sentence that is missing any of these elements will NOT be a complete sentence and does not express a complete thought. Incomplete sentences are unclear and confusing.

¡Atención! A complete sentence will answer the question *Who is doing what?* Look at the following sentence, for example:

1	2	3
Carmen y Jorge	**visitan**	**monumentos en Nuevo México.**

All three necessary elements are present, and we can answer the question *Who is doing what?* because this is a complete sentence. But if we eliminate one part, the sentence becomes unclear.

Visitan monumentos en Nuevo México. (*Who does?*)

Carmen y Jorge monumentos en Nuevo México. (*They do what? Visit them? Build them? Post reviews about them?*)

Carmen y Jorge visitan. (*Who or what are they visiting?*)

You can avoid writing incomplete and unclear sentences by making sure that each sentence you write contains all three elements and expresses a complete thought.

PRÁCTICA: Rewrite each sentence, adding the missing information so that it clearly answers the question *Who is doing what?*

1. José el videojuego de su hermano.
   ____
2. No vuelvo.
   ____
3. Tú y Miguel dos boletos, ¿verdad?
   ____
4. Tienen mucha prisa.
   ____
5. ¿Por qué no cierras?
   ____
6. Pilar y yo para ver el partido.
   ____
7. Sigue el sendero.
   ____
8. El béisbol es.
   ____
9. La iglesia católica en la Avenida Zapata.
   ____
10. Duermen en el autobús.
   ____

11. Los turistas quieren ir.

12. Marco con Rosa a las dos.

13. Ponemos.

14. Celia entiende.

15. ¿Va al café ahora?

16. Tú una revista en español.

17. Mamá siempre dice.

7

La próxima oración Write a sentence that might logically follow each sentence below. Make your sentence related to but different from the sentence given. Be sure the sentence you write has a clear subject and a verb and that it expresses a complete though. Follow the model.

modelo

Jaime juega muy bien al fútbol.
YOU WRITE, FOR EXAMPLE: *Su equipo gana muchos partidos.*

1. A Sara le gustan las montañas.

2. Hoy no podemos escribir mensajes electrónicos.

3. Leo el periódico a veces (*at times*).

4. Mi hermana perezosa toma el sol.

5. Yolanda piensa en su novio.

6. Gonzalo y Víctor pasan los ratos libres en casa.

7. La piscina municipal está lejos de nuestra casa.

8. El niño no quiere ir al museo.

9. Traigo un sándwich al parque.

10. Nina no recuerda muchas palabras del vocabulario.

11. Pepe no puede conseguir boletos para el partido de béisbol.

12. El restaurante Metrópolis está en la plaza central.

13. Los turistas tienen mucha hambre.

14. No me gusta el esquí acuático porque es muy peligroso (*dangerous*).

15. Carla mira la televisión hasta las tres de la mañana.

8 **El cuento de Eduardo** ETAPA 1: LEER In the following story, Eduardo writes about his family's pastimes. Review the glossed words first, and then read the story at least two times. If there are any parts you do not understand, underline or highlight them.

Los sábados son siempre° un día de mucha actividad. Mi hermana Lisa tiene la clase de piano a las nueve, y mi hermano Sergio tiene que llegar al estadio municipal para su partido de fútbol a las nueve y cuarto. Después°, al mediodía, los dos toman una clase de karate. A veces° a papá le gusta jugar al golf para descansar. Mamá va al centro para comprar las cosas que necesitamos en casa, y a las tres juega a las cartas o al dominó con unas amigas. Yo dedico el día a practicar tenis, andar en patineta o hacer el montón (¿o es una montaña?) de tarea que nos asigna la malévola° profesora de literatura americana. Casi nunca° puedo pasar los ratos libres solo y tranquilo. A las seis vamos todos a un restaurante para cenar, o pedimos una pizza enorme y comemos en casa. Por la noche jugamos a los videojuegos o vemos una película. Cuando es hora de acostarse°, todos tenemos sueño.

siempre *always* Después *Afterward* A veces *Sometimes* malévola *evil* Casi nunca *Almost never* hora de acostarse *time to go to bed*

Nombre ______________________ Fecha ______________________

ETAPA 2: EXAMINAR Go back through the story and find six words for each category listed: **Sustantivos, Verbos, Adjetivos, Cognados** (*Cognates*), and **Expresiones temporales** (*Time expressions*).

Sustantivos	Verbos	Adjetivos
1. ______	1. ______	1. ______
2. ______	2. ______	2. ______
3. ______	3. ______	3. ______
4. ______	4. ______	4. ______
5. ______	5. ______	5. ______
6. ______	6. ______	6. ______

Cognados	Expresiones temporales
1. ______	1. ______
2. ______	2. ______
3. ______	3. ______
4. ______	4. ______
5. ______	5. ______
6. ______	6. ______

ETAPA 3: ESCRIBIR Now write six sentences of your own, using Eduardo's story as a model. Make your sentences personal, writing about people you know and real-life events. Use stem-changing verbs, the verb **ir**, and vocabulary related to leisure-time activities. Consult the checklist on page 87 to help you write complete sentences and to look for possible errors in them.

Tema (*Topic*): Los sábados son siempre un día de mucha actividad.

1. ____

2. ____

3. ____

4. ____

5. ____

6. ____

Nombre Fecha

9 **Mi agenda** Fill in the following day planner page to describe what you will do this week. Include at least two items for each day. Give details, including what time, with whom, why. Write complete sentences. Use each of the following verbs at least once.

deber + *inf.*	ir a + *inf.*	poder + *inf.*
desear + *inf.*	necesitar + *inf.*	querer + *inf.*
esperar + *inf.*	pensar + *inf.*	tener que + *inf.*

LUNES:

MARTES:

MIÉRCOLES:

JUEVES:

VIERNES:

SÁBADO:

DOMINGO:

Nombre ______________________ Fecha ______________________

10 **¡Escríbelo!** Complete the following writing tasks. When writing sentences, remember to include details that make them more interesting. For example, don't just write **Vamos al cine**. Add more information: **Vamos al cine a ver una película de Casey Affleck.**

1. **a.** Write a short dialogue (five to six lines) between you and an adult you know about a trip he/she is taking soon. First, brainstorm some ideas for your dialogue on a separate piece of paper.

   b. Now write your dialogue below. Set up your dialogue following the model.

modelo

Yo: Hola, Sr. Vega. ¿Ud. ...?

Sr. Vega: Sí, es verdad. Voy a...

____

____

____

____

____

____

2. **a.** Write five sentences to tell what you and your friends/family are going to do next month (**el mes próximo**). Draw an idea map on a separate piece of paper to organize your ideas before you write. (You can review the use of idea maps on page 108 in **Lección 3**.)

   b. Now write your sentences below.

____

____

____

____

____

____

3. **a.** Write five to six sentences about things you do on a rainy weekend. Organize your ideas by making a list or drawing a mind map on a separate piece of paper.

   b. Now write your sentences below.

____

____

____

____

____

____

Nombre ______________________ Fecha ______________________

11 **Repaso del vocabulario** By studying **Lecciones 1–4** you have already learned a few hundred words and expressions in Spanish. Not bad! Now let's see how many you remember.

ETAPA 1: Fill in the following chart without looking in your textbook. When you finish, check to make sure each word is spelled correctly and that all accents are in place.

A. Outdoor activities	
1. ______	6. ______
2. ______	7. ______
3. ______	8. ______
4. ______	9. ______
5. ______	10. ______

B. Indoor activities	
1. ______	6. ______
2. ______	7. ______
3. ______	8. ______
4. ______	9. ______
5. ______	10. ______

C. Words to describe a good friend of yours (appearance and personality)	
1. ______	6. ______
2. ______	7. ______
3. ______	8. ______
4. ______	9. ______
5. ______	10. ______

D. Words that indicate members of your family	
1. ______	6. ______
2. ______	7. ______
3. ______	8. ______
4. ______	9. ______
5. ______	10. ______

Nombre ______________________ Fecha ______________________

E. Things you find in your backpack or locker	
1.	6.
2.	7.
3.	8.
4.	9.
5.	10.

F. Places you like to go	
1.	6.
2.	7.
3.	8.
4.	9.
5.	10.

G. Professions or careers	
1.	6.
2.	7.
3.	8.
4.	9.
5.	10.

H. Subjects you don't like in school	
1.	6.
2.	7.
3.	8.
4.	9.
5.	10.

I. Things you usually do after school	
1.	6.
2.	7.
3.	8.
4.	9.
5.	10.

Nombre ______________________ Fecha ______________________

ETAPA 2: Your teacher will pick a number from 1 to 10. Use the word or expression you wrote in that numbered space of each chart A through I and write a complete sentence. Consult the checklist on page 87 to help you write complete sentences and to look for possible errors in them.

modelo

Imagine your teacher picks number 4. In section A, Outdoor activities, you have written **jugar al golf** *in space 4. You then write a sentence using* **jugar al golf**.
For example: El Sr. Rosas juega al golf en Pebble Beach.

A. ______________________

B. ______________________

C. ______________________

D. ______________________

E. ______________________

F. ______________________

G. ______________________

H. ______________________

I. ______________________

Nombre ______________________ Fecha ______________________

Lección 5

1 **Sopa de letras** Find 25 vocabulary words from **Lección 5** in the grid, looking horizontally, vertically, or diagonally. Circle them in the puzzle and put a check mark next to the clue in the list below. **¡Buena suerte!** (*Good luck!*)

```
S I D L L A V E R F L O V C
C U R T Ó N G A G E N C I A
A O C A M P R S E L P U N M
N Q U I N T A B U I A P J A
S Y E G O L S O N Z S A B E
A E C R I T C E L R A D A L
D W H D É P E Q U I P A J E
A M A B L E N U R V O S A G
B E M O J I S C E R R A D O
S A C A R F O T O S T L V N
D N O B Ú T R E X R E E I F
O F R P L A Y A T E R C E R
B O T O N E S B O M K C N Í
L Q H U M O R X Á C H O T O
E P R I M A V E R A I N O L
```

1. número 5 = la ________
2. el 3 de marzo, por ejemplo
3. Ella quiere dormir porque está ________.
4. Hace ________ en invierno.
5. No es la llegada; es la ________.
6. donde duermes
7. En un hotel, él lleva las maletas.
8. Usas una cámara para ________. (2 palabras)
9. para ir al décimo piso
10. las maletas = el ________
11. habitación para dos personas
12. documento necesario para viajar
13. estación de las flores (*flowers*)
14. cosa que abre la puerta
15. alegre
16. lo opuesto de **limpio**
17. ________ de viajes
18. simpático
19. no está abierto
20. después del segundo
21. de buen ________
22. Ellas tienen mucho que hacer. Están ________.
23. Chicago es la cuidad del ________.
24. la planta ________
25. al lado del mar

2 **Familias de palabras** The first word(s) in each group is an expression you have learned. What do you think the new words in boldface mean? Write their English meaning in the space.

1. el/la empleado/a	**el empleo** [*noun*]	______
2. el año	**anual** [*adjective*]	______
3. el hotel	**el/la hotelero/a** [*person*]	______
4. confirmar	**la confirmación** [*noun*]	______
5. la reservación	**reservar** [*verb*]	______
6. el/la inspector(a)	**la inspección** [*noun*]	______
	inspeccionar [*verb*]	______
7. confundido/a	**confundir a alguien** (*someone*) [*verb*]	______
8. alegre	**la alegría** [*noun*]	______
9. las vacaciones	**vacacionar** [*verb*]	______
10. llover (llueve)	**la lluvia** [*noun*]	______
11. nevar (nieve)	**la nieve** [*noun*]	______
12. el sol (hace sol)	**solar** [*adjective*]	______
13. nervioso/a	**los nervios** [*noun*]	______
14. las fotos	**fotográfico/a** [*adjective*]	______
	el/la fotógrafo/a [*person*]	______
15. limpio/a	**limpiar** [*verb*]	______
16. enojado/a	**el enojo** [*noun*]	______

3 **Asociaciones** ETAPA 1: Using the following topics as a starting point, write a few related words or phrases that you associate with each one. The purpose here is to generate ideas and insights you have about each topic. There are no wrong answers.

1. las vacaciones perfectas ______________________________
____
____
____

2. Estoy aburrido/a cuando… ______________________________
____
____
____

3. mi estación favorita ______________________________
____
____
____

ETAPA 2: Now, using the ideas you generated in **Etapa 1**, write three to four complete sentences about each topic using the ideas you brainstormed. Consult the checklist on page 87 to help you write complete sentences and to look for possible errors in them.

1. a. ______________________________
   b. ______________________________
   c. ______________________________
   d. ______________________________

2. a. ______________________________
   b. ______________________________
   c. ______________________________
   d. ______________________________

3. a. ______________________________
   b. ______________________________
   c. ______________________________
   d. ______________________________

4 **¿Lógico o ilógico?** Read each sentence and decide if it makes sense or not. If it does, write Es lógico. If it does not, rewrite the sentence so it does make sense.

modelo

La agencia de viajes está equivocada los domingos.
YOU WRITE, FOR EXAMPLE: *La agencia de viajes está cerrada los domingos.*

1. Carlos nada en el estación de tren.
2. Alfredo necesita un equipaje de ida y vuelta.
3. Está lloviendo y vamos a esquiar en la montaña.
4. Ana sonríe porque está de mal humor.
5. Hace muy buen tiempo y por eso (*so*) pasamos unas horas en la playa.
6. Los turistas están enojados con el paisaje.
7. Para ir al centro, los Sres. Galván montan a caballo.
8. El hotel sirve comida internacional en una cama en la planta baja.
9. Necesitamos tomar el ascensor al noveno piso.
10. Antonia y Elena buscan un agente de viajes para llevar sus maletas a la habitación.
11. Ustedes van de compras ahora mismo en las aduanas, ¿verdad?
12. Mercedes pone su pasaporte y su pasaje en su viento.
13. Los padres de Roberto viven en la fecha y están muy felices.
14. Los viajeros quieren hacer surf y nadar en el mar.
15. Amalia confirma las cartas en línea (*online*).
16. Necesitas una llave doble para dos personas.

5 **Reescribir** Rewrite each sentence below, substituting new information for the underlined words. Follow the model.

modelo

Paloma <u>va en taxi</u> al centro.
YOU WRITE, FOR EXAMPLE: *Paloma camina al centro.*
or *Paloma corre al centro.*
or *Paloma toma el metro al centro.*

1. Ignacio no quiere <u>ir al museo</u> hoy.
______
2. Rafa y Javier <u>hacen las maletas</u>.
______
3. <u>El empleado</u> está de muy mal humor.
______
4. Necesitamos dos <u>habitaciones dobles</u>.
______
5. Mis padres pasan el invierno <u>en Puerto Rico</u>.
______
6. Oye, ¡vas a <u>perder el autobús</u>!
______
7. En junio Teresa viaja <u>en barco a Europa</u>.
______
8. <u>La agente de viajes</u> confirma las reservaciones para nosotros.
______
9. <u>La planta baja del hotel</u> está muy sucia y desordenada.
______
10. Vivo <u>cerca del mar</u> porque me gusta nadar.
______
11. ¡Selena y Celia están <u>enamoradas del mismo hombre</u>!
______
12. La primavera <u>empieza el 21 de marzo en Norteamérica</u>.
______
13. Los viajeros esperan la llegada <u>del tren de Monterrey</u>.
______
14. Consuelo está contenta porque <u>le gusta mucho el restaurante</u>.
______
15. Muchos turistas pierden <u>la llave de su habitación</u>.
______

6 **La próxima oración** Write a sentence that might logically follow each sentence below. Make your sentence related to but different from the sentence given. Be sure the sentence you write has a clear subject and a verb and that it expresses a complete thought. Follow the model.

modelo

Rosario no puede cerrar su maleta.
YOU WRITE, FOR EXAMPLE: *Su marido dice que van a perder el tren si no salen ahora mismo.*

1. No estudio esta noche porque está nevando.
2. ¡El empleado no encuentra la reservación de Verónica en la computadora!
3. Los sábados juego a las cartas con mis amigos.
4. ¡NO… estás equivocado/a!
5. Jacinta se niega a (*refuses to*) ir a acampar con su novio.
6. Rodrigo y Felipe buscan las tablas de surf en el garaje.
7. Los dos restaurantes están muy ocupados.
8. Tu cuarto parece muy desordenado.
9. Paso las vacaciones en la playa.
10. El Sr. Rojas está confundido.
11. Paloma y Orlando tienen una habitación doble muy bonita.
12. La escuela está cerrada por dos días.
13. Llueve y hace fresco.
14. Uds. deben esperar hasta (*until*) el otoño para ir a San Juan.
15. El autobús sale a las siete de la mañana.

7

Estrategia: *Using* porque *to provide additional information* One way to add information to a sentence is to explain *why* someone does something or feels a certain way. Look at the following two sentences:

Ernesto acampa en el Parque Yellowstone.

Carolina está triste.

Both of these sentences are perfectly correct the way they are: each contains a clear subject, a verb, and enough additional information to express a complete thought.

However, if you want to add even more information and impact to them, you can ask the question **¿Por qué? ¿Por qué acampa Ernesto en el Parque Yellowstone? ¿Por qué está triste Carolina?**

To answer those questions, add the connecting word **porque** to the end of the sentence and then give the reason. Note that the reason also has to be expressed as a complete sentence.

complete sentence + **porque** + reason (complete sentence)

Ernesto acampa en el Parque Yellowstone **porque** quiere sacar fotos de las montañas.

Carolina está triste **porque** sus padres dicen que ella no puede ir al concierto.

PRÁCTICA 1: Use **porque** to add a reason to each of the following statements. Follow the model.

modelo

Elena no va a la playa.

YOU WRITE, FOR EXAMPLE: Elena no va a la playa porque tiene que estudiar.

1. Rodrigo está cantando. ______________________
2. Los Pérez salen mañana. ______________________
3. Tengo frío. ______________________
4. Uds. no montan a caballo. ______________________
5. No queremos una habitación en el décimo piso. ______________________

PRÁCTICA 2: Now write a sentence that goes before **porque** and each reason given. Follow the model.

modelo

porque tiene que estudiar

YOU WRITE, FOR EXAMPLE: Elena no va a la playa porque tiene que estudiar.

1. porque el restaurante cierra a las diez ______________________
2. porque su hermano está de vacaciones ______________________
3. porque está lloviendo ______________________
4. porque el profesor no viene hoy ______________________
5. porque a Fernando no le gusta viajar en avión ______________________

Nombre ______________________ Fecha ______________________

Lección 5

8 **Un día en el hotel** Read the brief description of each hotel. Then write a few sentences about each one: when you think tourists typically go there, what the weather is like, the activities offered, amenities, and so on. The following words may be useful.

lujoso/a, de lujo *luxurious*
el servicio de habitación *room service*
generalmente *generally*
conexión WiFi gratis *free WiFi connection*

1. **El Chalé Nieves:** Hotel-chalé° tradicional, cómodo y cerca de las pistas° para el aficionado al esquí

2. **El Balneario° Mar Bello:** Hotel y spa de lujo con suites y estudios bien equipados°, servicios para consentir° a todo turista

3. **El Hotel Pulgas°:** ¡Barato°, barato, barato!

chalé *chalet, mountain lodge* pistas *ski slopes* Balneario *Health resort, spa* estudios bien equipados *fully equipped studio apartments* consentir *to spoil* Pulgas *Fleas* Barato *Cheap*

Nombre ____________________ Fecha ____________________

9 **El viaje de Marisol** **ETAPA 1: LEER** In the following story, Marisol writes about her first vacation without her family. Review the glossed words first, and then read the story at least two times. If there are any parts you do not understand, underline or highlight them.

[1] En junio, Marisol tiene un viaje a Puerto Rico, y es la primera vez° que sale de vacaciones con sus amigas y no con sus padres. [2] Tiene un poco de° miedo y está un poco nerviosa, pero también está muy entusiasmada°. [3] En cambio°, sus padres sí están muy preocupados... ¡y absolutamente prohíben que algún chico las acompañe!°

[4] Marisol y sus tres amigas reservan dos habitaciones dobles en un sitio web y reciben un descuento de 10 por ciento°. [5] Sus pasajes son un poco caros porque es la temporada alta° para viajar. [6] Cada° chica no puede traer más de° una maleta – van a tener que compartir algunas° cosas. [7] Después de llegar al aeropuerto en San Juan van a tomar un taxi o un autobús al hotel que está ubicado° directamente en la playa.

[8] El hotel tiene tres cafés, cuatro restaurantes excelentes, una boutique y un cine y ofrece muchas actividades. [*To be continued. . .*]

vez *time* un poco de *a little* entusiasmada *excited* En cambio *On the other hand* ¡y absolutamente... *and they absolutely forbid that any boys go with them* por ciento *percent* temporada alta *busy season, tourist season* Cada *Each* más de *more than* algunas *some* ubicado *located*

ETAPA 2: EXAMINAR Go back through the story and find six words for each category listed: **Sustantivos**, **Verbos**, and **Adjetivos**.

Sustantivos	Verbos	Adjetivos
1. ________	1. ________	1. ________
2. ________	2. ________	2. ________
3. ________	3. ________	3. ________
4. ________	4. ________	4. ________
5. ________	5. ________	5. ________
6. ________	6. ________	6. ________

ETAPA 3: RECONOCER COGNADOS What do you think the following Spanish words mean in English?

1. reservan (*sentence 4*) ____________________
2. un sitio web (*sentence 4*) ____________________
3. un descuento (*sentence 4*) ____________________
4. directamente (*sentence 7*) ____________________
5. una boutique (*sentence 8*) ____________________

ETAPA 4: ESCRIBIR Now you're the writer! It's up to you to finish the story. Write at least five more sentences about Marisol, her friends, and their vacation plans. Consult the checklist on page 87 to help you write complete sentences and to look for possible errors in them.

1. ______
2. ______
3. ______
4. ______
5. ______

10 **Estrategia: *Making an Outline*** An *outline* (**un esquema del texto**) is a way of summarizing information in a predictable format. Once you learn this format, you can easily make outlines of your class notes and use them to study for tests and your final exams. Making an outline of a text you've read helps you remember key points. And outlines help you organize your thoughts when you have to write a longer assignment, such as a report or term paper.

Review the **Escritura** on page 182 of your textbook before you practice making outlines in the activities that follow.

PRÁCTICA 1: Each group of phrases below contains a main topic and three subtopics. Mark the main topic with an **X**. Then, in the space provided, write an additional subtopic that fits logically in the group.

1. ____ montar a caballo en la playa
   ____ actividades que ofrece el hotel para niños
   ____ clases de natación y de surf
   ____ jugar al voleibol acuático
   additional subtopic: ______

2. ____ habitaciones con vista (*view*) al mar
   ____ guardias de seguridad
   ____ un hotel de 4 estrellas (*stars*)
   ____ dos restaurantes famosos
   additional subtopic: ______

3. _____ hace mucho frío
   _____ nieva todos los días
   _____ esquiar y patinar sobre hielo (*ice*)
   _____ el invierno
   additional subtopic: ______________________

4. _____ cómo llegar
   _____ alquilar (*rent*) un automóvil
   _____ viajar en avión
   _____ ir en bicicleta
   additional subtopic: ______________________

5. _____ un tour de San Juan
   _____ las playas de Vieques
   _____ las vacaciones en Puerto Rico
   _____ el Museo de la Música Puertorriqueña
   additional subtopic: ______________________

PRÁCTICA 2: You have been learning the present indicative tense of Spanish verbs since **Lección 1**, and you have learned the present progressive tense as well. Now you will create an outline of what you have learned about Spanish verbs so far.

Etapa 1: First, read the following outline headings, topics, and subtopics, and decide which ones are the most important (the headings). Write them in the uppercase letter spaces on the next page. The first one is done for you.

Outline headings, topics, and subtopics	
Irregular verbs: Those that do not follow regular patterns	Present participles that end in **-yendo**
Verbs with irregular present participles	Regular **-er** verbs
e to **i**	**ser**
estar	Verbs with regular present participles
Present participles of **-ir** stem-changing verbs	**e** to **ie**
Regular **-ar** verbs	Verbs with irregular **yo** forms
Regular **-ir** verbs	**tener** and **venir**
o to **ue**	**ir**
	~~Regular verbs: Those that follow regular patterns~~.

Etapa 2: Next, figure out which topics should come under each lettered item. Write them in the numbered spaces.

Etapa 3: Finally, fill in the remaining subtopics in the lowercase letter spaces.

Outline of Spanish Verbs

I. PRESENT INDICATIVE

A. Regular verbs: Those that follow regular patterns

1. ______________________
2. ______________________
3. ______________________

B. ______________________

1. ______________________
2. ______________________
3. ______________________
4. ______________________
5. Stem-changing verbs
    a. ______________________
    b. ______________________
    c. ______________________
6. ______________________

II. PRESENT PROGRESSIVE

A. ______________________

B. ______________________

1. ______________________
2. ______________________

Nombre ______________________ Fecha ______________________

11 **Esquema de texto: Puerto Rico** ETAPA 1: Using information from the chapter's **Panorama** on Puerto Rico, create an outline. Use the following headings and add topics and subtopics as needed.

I. Información general sobre la isla
II. Ciudades importantes
III. El Morro
IV. La salsa
V. Historia: 1898 al presente

Lección 5

Nombre ______________________ Fecha ______________________

ETAPA 2: Now choose another **Panorama** country from the **Senderos 1** text and create an outline for it:

Lección 2: España

Lección 3: Ecuador

Lección 4: México

You must write your own headings this time. Use the outlines you've worked on so far as a model.

Tema de mi borrador (*draft*): ______________________

Nombre ______________________ Fecha ______________________

Lección 6

1 **Crucigrama** Solve the following crossword puzzle with words and expressions from this chapter.

HORIZONTAL

1. para las manos
4. Cuando vas a un concierto, compras una ________ de recuerdo y te la pones.
8. Ella ________ del inglés al español.
10. No es caro; es ________.
11. los vestidos de seda (*silk*) lo son
12. la mezcla (*mixture*) del rojo con el azul
14. Su sombrero hace ________ con su vestido.
16. bonito
19. estas, esas y ________
20. la ropa ________
22. los llevas con los zapatos
23. manera conveniente de pagar: con ________ (3 palabras)

VERTICAL

1. Y tú, ¿cuánto ________? ¿Cincuenta dólares?
2. Macy's y JCPenney, por ejemplo
3. ¿Quién ________ la respuesta?
4. trajes, camisas y ________
5. café
6. Cuando hace fresco, llevas un ________.
7. el color que resulta de mezclar (*mix*) el rojo con el amarillo
9. No es el dependiente; es un ________.
13. un abrigo ligero (*light*)
15. sinónimo de **llevar**
17. hace dos días (*two days ago*)
18. No regateas cuando los precios son ________.
21. No es corto; es ________.

Nombre ______________________ Fecha ______________________

2 **Familias de palabras** ETAPA 1: The first word(s) in each group is an expression you have learned. What do you think the new words in boldface mean? Write their English meaning in the space.

1. costar — **el coste** *or* **el costo** [*noun*] ______________________
2. la rebaja — **rebajado/a** [*adjective*] ______________________
3. pobre — **la pobreza** [*noun*] ______________________
4. vender
   el/la vendedor(a) — **la venta** [*noun*] ______________________
5. pagar — **el pago** [*noun*] ______________________
6. el regalo — **regalar** [*verb*] ______________________
7. loco/a — **la locura** [*noun*] ______________________
8. ofrecer — **una oferta** [*noun*] ______________________
9. rico/a — **la riqueza** [*noun*] ______________________
10. el color — **colorear** [*verb*] ______________________
11. pasado/a — **el pasado** [*noun*] ______________________
12. traducir — **el/la traductor(a)** [*person*] ______________________
    la traducción [*noun*] ______________________

ETAPA 2: Answer the following questions:.

1. If you know the word **guantes,** can you guess the meaning of **el guante de béisbol**?

   ____

2. If you know the word **cinturón,** can you guess the meaning of **el cinturón de seguridad**? (**Pista:** You find them on airplanes and in cars.)

   ____

3. If you know what a **tarjeta de crédito** is, can you figure out what a **tarjeta de débito** might be?

   ____

4. You've learned the word **traje.** Picture it in your mind. What do you think a **traje de tres piezas** is?

   ____

   El traje de tres piezas consists of **una chaqueta, unos pantalones,** and **un chaleco.** What do you think **un chaleco** is?

   ____

Lección 6

Nombre ______ Fecha ______

3 **Reescribir** Rewrite each sentence below, substituting new information for the underlined words. If the original sentence uses a preterite verb, make sure your new sentence is also in the preterite. Follow the model.

modelo

Ana y Raquel nos enseñaron español.

YOU WRITE, FOR EXAMPLE: Ana y Raquel aprendieron español.

or Ana y Raquel hablaron español.

1. Nicolás compró un traje elegante.
2. Diego y Alejandra regatearon con los vendedores.
3. El dependiente nos mostró una bolsa muy cara.
4. La semana pasada leímos una novela muy larga.
5. Esos pantalones no hacen juego con esa camisa. (*2 substitutions*)
6. Oye, ¿cuánto dinero gastaste en aquella tienda?
7. Ayer Matías pagó cien dólares por un par de zapatos.
8. Manuela sabe preparar la comida cubana.
9. Mi abuela siempre me da muchos besos y abrazos.
10. No conozco a esos clientes. ¿Cómo se llaman?
11. Viviana necesita comprar un vestido nuevo para la boda (*wedding*).
12. El centro comercial de Camagüey cerró a las diez de la noche.
13. ¿Cuántas blusas vendió Ud. ayer, Sra. Morales?
14. Camila me prestó su suéter rosado.
15. Consuelo y su madre buscaron una falda hermosa pero barata.
16. Prefiero los mercados al aire libre a los almacenes. (*2 substitutions*)
17. ¡Jimena dejó (*left*) su tarjeta de crédito en la mesa del café!

Nombre ______________________ Fecha ______________________

4 **Temas** Write at least five sentences about each of the following topics. Consult the checklist on page 87 to help you write complete sentences and to look for possible errors in them.

1. Write a short dialogue between two or three people on the first day of the school year.

2. Write about the clothes and supplies you need (or want) to buy for school.

3. Describe a member of your family that you admire and tell why.

4. Say what the people around you are doing right now (**ahora mismo**).

5. Talk about what a lazy student does on the weekend.

6. Now say what a hard-working student does in her/his free time.

7. Finally, write about what you did yesterday, last week, a month ago, etc.

5 **Estrategia: *Writing Sentences with* cuando *Clauses*** In Lección 5 of this workbook you wrote sentences that added information by answering the question **¿Por qué?** Another way to add information is to use the conjunction, or joining word, **cuando** (*when* or *whenever*). **Cuando** expresses a condition or supplies an explanation.

Let's use one of the example sentences from **Lección 5**:

Ernesto acampa en el Parque Yellowstone.

You can place a **cuando** clause at the end of this sentence to add more information:

Ernesto acampa en el Parque Yellowstone **cuando hace buen tiempo.**
Ernesto camps at Yellowstone Park when it's nice weather.

or

Ernesto acampa en el Parque Yellowstone **cuando tiene tiempo libre.**
Ernesto camps at Yellowstone Park whenever he has free time.

You can also move the clause that begins with **cuando** to the beginning of the sentence and add a comma. This is another way to vary your word order to make some sentences stand out.

Cuando hace buen tiempo, Ernesto acampa en el Parque Yellowstone.
Cuando tiene tiempo libre, Ernesto acampa en el Parque Yellowstone.

As with **porque**, you use a complete sentence after the word **cuando**.

PRÁCTICA 1: Rewrite each of the following sentences, adding a **cuando** clause to the end of it. Follow the model.

modelo

Yo sé todas las respuestas.
YOU WRITE, FOR EXAMPLE: *Yo sé todas las respuestas cuando estudio mucho.*

1. Juliana está triste. ____________________
2. Mariela siempre quiere ropa nueva. ____________________
3. Los dependientes llegan tarde al almacén. ____________________
4. Los Tigres pierden muchos partidos. ____________________
5. Hay rebajas en esta tienda. ____________________

6. El Sr. Olivares lleva traje y corbata. ______

7. Compramos camisetas y pantalones cortos. ______

8. Los chicos venden sus bicicletas. ______

9. Jorge busca su tarjeta de crédito. ______

10. ¿Qué dices? ______

PRÁCTICA 2: Now, rewrite the sentences you created in **Práctica 1** moving the **cuando** clause to the beginning. Remember to put a comma at the end of the **cuando** clause. Consult the checklist on page 87 to help you write complete sentences and to look for possible errors in them.

modelo

YOU WROTE: Yo sé todas las respuestas cuando estudio mucho.
YOUR NEW SENTENCE: *Cuando estudio mucho, yo sé todas las respuestas.*

1. ______
2. ______
3. ______
4. ______
5. ______
6. ______
7. ______
8. ______
9. ______
10. ______

6

Estrategia: *Combining Your Sentence-Writing Strategies* In this workbook you have learned several strategies for writing sentences in Spanish:

- verifying that every sentence has a clear subject, a verb, and enough information to express a complete thought (p. 15)
- varying word order for impact (p. 40)
- adding information and details using **porque** (p. 65)
- adding information and details using a **cuando** clause (p. 78)

Now it's time to practice all of these strategies to see how they can improve your sentence writing skills.

PRÁCTICA 1: Read each sentence carefully to make sure it has (**a**) a clear subject, (**b**) a verb that agrees with the subject, *and* (**c**) enough information to express a complete thought. If it does, put a checkmark next to it. If it does not, rewrite it and make any adjustments necessary so that you have a complete sentence.

1. Isabel en el centro comercial.

   ____

2. Edgardo no conoce.

   ____

3. Esos clientes compraron zapatos y calcetines.

   ____

4. Su vestido azul no muy elegante.

   ____

5. Buscó su maleta en el aeropuerto pero no la encontró.

   ____

6. La semana pasada pagué.

   ____

7. Lo siento, pero no conduces muy bien.

   ____

8. No costaron mucho.

   ____

9. Estudiaron Héctor.

   ____

10. Esa dependienta vendió cuatro bolsas muy caras ayer.

    ____

11. Uds. no saben, ¿verdad?

    ____

12. La tarjeta de crédito y el pasaporte.

    ____

PRÁCTICA 2: Change each of the following sentences in three ways. On line **A**, vary the word order so the subject does not come first. On line **B**, add **porque** and an explanation. On line **C**, add a **cuando** clause, either at the beginning or at the end of the sentence. Use the model as a guide.

modelo

Andrea compra una blusa y una falda.

A. *Compra Andrea una blusa y una falda. or*
Una blusa y una falda compra Andrea.

B. *Andrea compra una blusa y una falda porque va a una fiesta.*

C. *Andrea compra una blusa y una falda cuando hay rebajas.*

1. La Sra. Roche paga en efectivo.
   A. ____________
   B. ____________
   C. ____________

2. Elliot pasea en bicicleta.
   A. ____________
   B. ____________
   C. ____________

3. Hilda y Patricia almuerzan en el Café Luna.
   A. ____________
   B. ____________
   C. ____________

4. Tú vas a necesitar cinco cuadernos, una mochila y dinero para libros.
   A. ____________
   B. ____________
   C. ____________

Lección 6

5. Nosotros salimos temprano (*early*).

A. ______________________________

B. ______________________________

____

C. ______________________________

____

6. Mariana no gasta mucho dinero.

A. ______________________________

B. ______________________________

____

C. ______________________________

____

7. Mi padre mira los deportes en la televisión.

A. ______________________________

B. ______________________________

____

C. ______________________________

____

7 **Repaso: Mapas de ideas** ETAPA 1: Create two **mapas de ideas** below about any topics you wish. Begin by writing your topics in the center shaded bubbles. Then add at least five ideas related to each topic. You may also add additional bubbles to include details.

A.

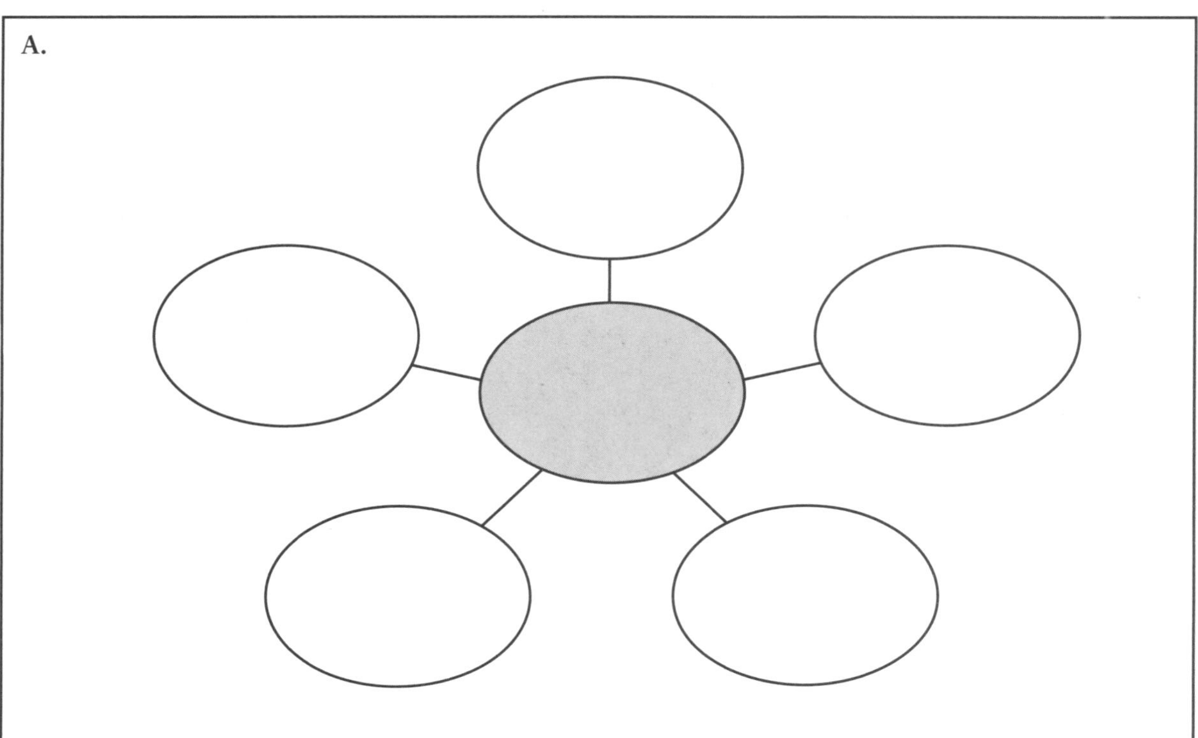

B.

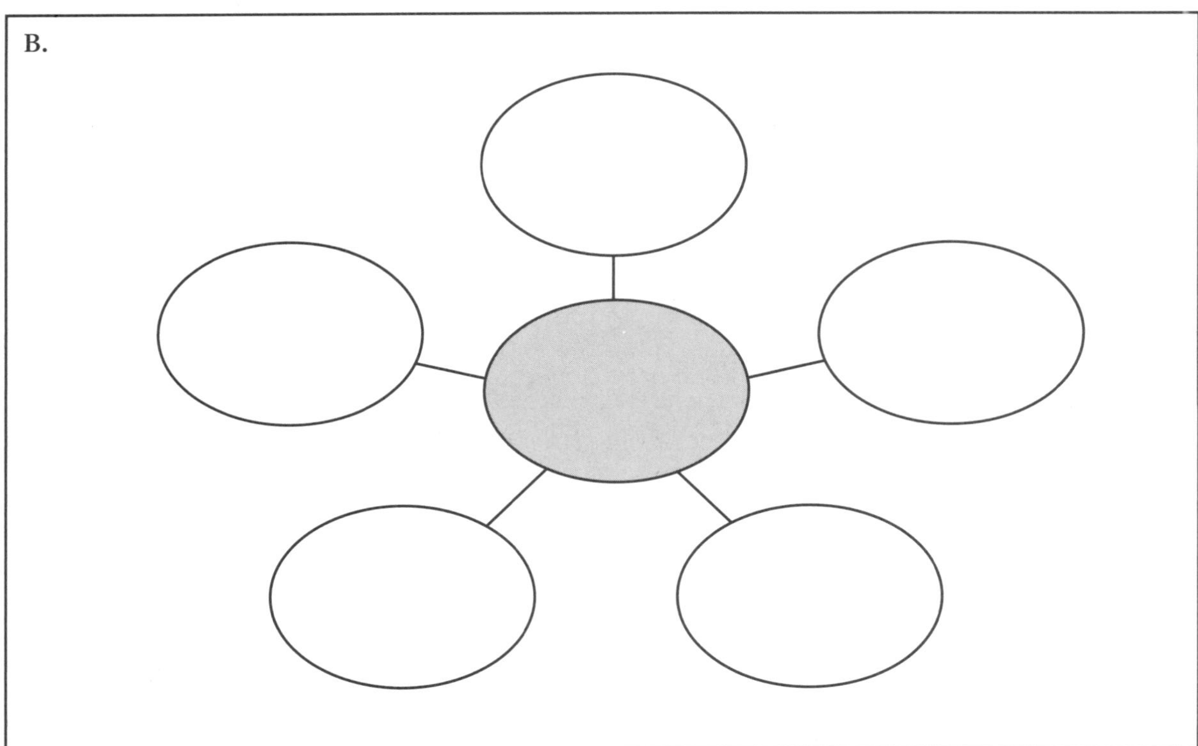

Nombre ______________________ Fecha ______________________

ETAPA 2: Now, using the ideas you generated in your **mapas de ideas** in **Etapa 1**, write at least five complete sentences about each topic. Your topic (**Tu tema**) comes from the shaded bubble in the middle. Write some of your sentences using the preterite of regular verbs, and include demonstrative adjectives and pronouns where possible. Consult the checklist on page 87 for help with writing correct sentences.

A. Tu tema: ______________________

1. ______________________

2. ______________________

3. ______________________

4. ______________________

5. ______________________

B. Tu tema: ______________________

1. ______________________

2. ______________________

3. ______________________

4. ______________________

5. ______________________

Nombre Fecha

8 **Un viaje de fin de semana** ETAPA 1: You will write about a weekend trip. Organize your ideas in an outline. Use the three main topics listed below and include at least one more. Fill in the subtopics and details that tell about the trip you are planning. Before you begin, review the outlining activities in **Lección 5** of this workbook (pages 71 and 72), as well as the **Escritura** "Making an Outline" strategy on page 182 of the **Senderos 1** textbook.

modelo

I. ¿Quiénes van?
  A. Marta
    1. compañera de clase y amiga
    2. muy divertida
  B. Mi papá
    1. va a conducir
    2. me da dinero
    etc.

I. ¿Quiénes van?
II. ¿Adónde vamos y qué hacemos allá?
III. ¿Qué traemos? (ropa, etc.)
IV. *Your own original topic*

Lección 6

ETAPA 2: Now turn each section of your outline into a series of complete sentences.

modelo

I. ¿Quiénes van?

Marta es una compañera de clase y mi amiga. Tiene que ir conmigo porque es muy divertida. También mi papá va con nosotros porque me da dinero…

Writing Checklist for Level 1 Use the following checklists to review your written work before turning it in.

Writing Words

- ✓ Are all words spelled correctly? Do words that require an accent have the accent in place over the correct vowel?
- ✓ Are cognates spelled correctly in Spanish?
- ✓ Are nouns paired with an appropriate definite or indefinite article that agrees in gender and number?
- ✓ Do adjectives agree with the nouns they modify in gender and number?
- ✓ If you have any "problem words" (words you often spell incorrectly, including mistakes with accents), write them here and be sure you spell them correctly in your writing assignments.

____

____

____

Writing Sentences

- ✓ Is each sentence punctuated correctly, with an inverted ¿ before a question and an inverted ¡ before an exclamation?
- ✓ Does each sentence contain a subject and a verb?
- ✓ Does each verb refer to a clearly understood subject?
- ✓ Does each verb agree in number and person with its subject?
- ✓ Is your sentence a fragment, or does it express a complete thought? Is there enough information included so that the sentence makes sense?
- ✓ Have you varied the word order of any of your sentences? If so, does it follow one of the patterns you learned on page 40?
- ✓ Have you added information or details to some of your sentences using **porque** or **cuando**?

Photography and Art Credits
All images © Vista Higher Learning unless otherwise noted.

Writing Proficiency Workbook
30: Ra2studio/Shutterstock; **51:** Media Bakery RF.

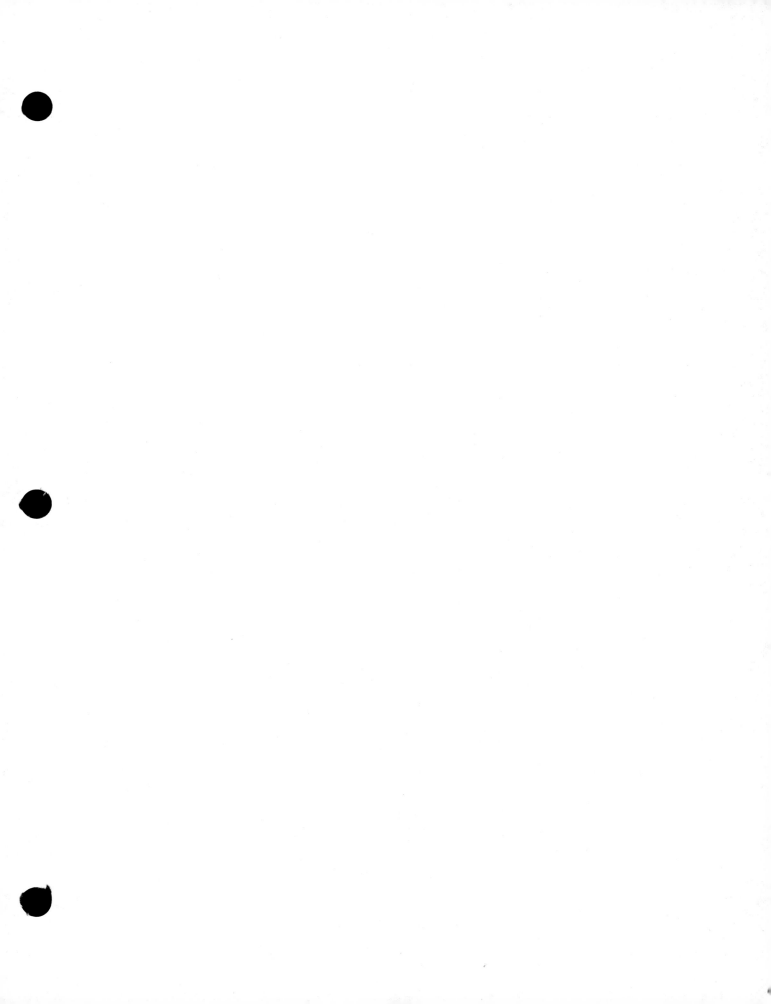